How a Computer Works

Copyright © 2015 Camboard Technology

Camboard Technology

Cambridge England

www.camboard.com

Age range 11+

Learn more about how a computer works.

How a Computer Works is a guide and reference tool. Packed with stunning graphics this guide brings the inside of a Windows PC to life.

A fascinating and absorbing overview of what's happening inside a computer.

Useful to students or those wishing to learn the mysterious operation of How a Computer Works. The book delves into the operation of the key components of a personal computer. The computers key processes are described in short form. Includes clear diagrams of the main computer parts. The heart of any computer is the CPU the book explains with clear diagrams the internal operation of an Intel Pentium processor. Includes comprehensive guides to the main components of your computer. Explains the technologies that make up a computer. Explains where all the connections on the back go to. Because so many Schools and educational establishments use older machines, this book is based on a Windows personal computer with an Intel Pentium processor, the boot up sequence described is for Windows XP and earlier versions. If you are going to take apart a computer too look inside.

DISCONNECT THE SYSTEM FROM THE MAINS ELECTRICITY FIRST!

Includes 28 chapters which explain the mystery of these technologies:-

Motherboard

PCI Bus

The power on self-test

BOOT Up

CPU

Memory

Hard Drive

CD-ROM

Modem

Printer

Interrupts

FireWire

Expansion Cards

Serial and Parallel Ports

BIOS

Plug and Play

Mouse

Keyboard

Floppy Disk

USB

Scanner

Sound

MIDI

SCSI

Monitor

Use of a term in this book should not be regarded as affecting the validity of any trademark, registered trademark, or service mark.

Camboard Technology is not associated with any product or vendor mentioned in this book.

All trademarks acknowledged

® Microsoft Windows is a registered trademark of Microsoft Corporation.

® Pentium is a registered trademark of Intel Corporation.

Contents

1. Introduction

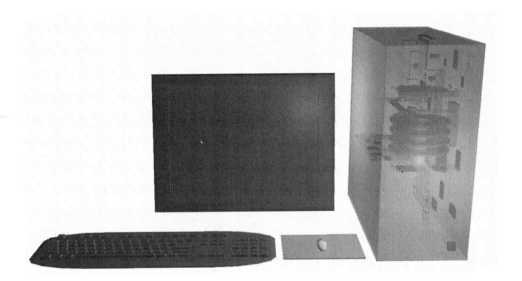

Personal Computer

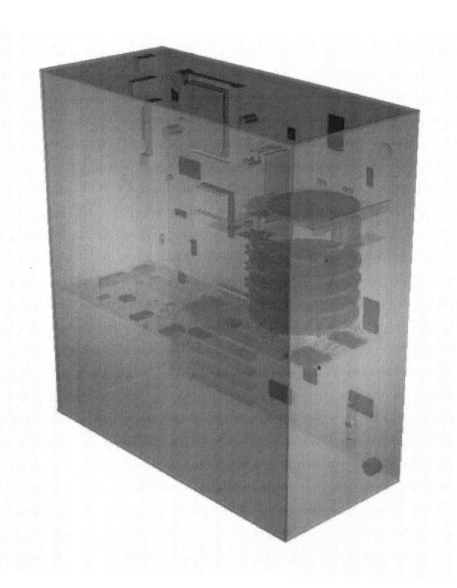

The P.C (Personal Computer) allows many tasks to be
undertaken which would otherwise not be possible.
From typing a letter to surfing the net the computers
versatility has meant many homes and workplaces rely

on the computer for everyday tasks. This book delves into the mysterious world of how the computer actually works inside those boxes. Although understanding the precise operation of computer hardware requires detailed technical knowledge, understanding the basics of how a computer works does not.

System Tower

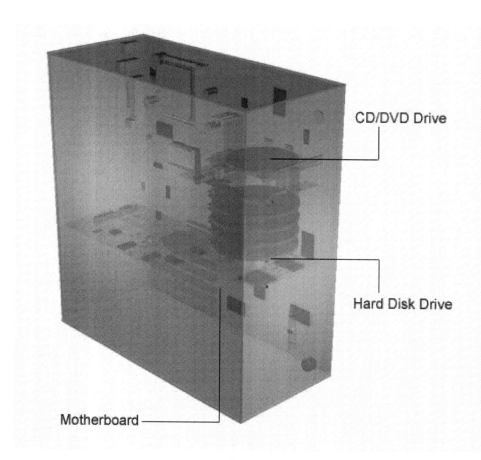

CD/DVD Drive

Hard Disk Drive

Motherboard

The computer system comprises of several boxes. The main computer is housed in a rectangle box. Inside this box is the motherboard and disk drives.

The drives connect to the motherboard through special ribbon cable. The cable contains many separate wires moulded into a flat wide cable.

Monitor

The monitor is housed in a separate box and plugs into the main system box.

Today's slim line monitors are a far cry from the old large cumbersome cathode ray tube monitors.

Keyboard

Mouse and Mat

The Keyboard and Mouse are housed in smaller boxes that connect to the main system box.

They connect either with a cable to the main system box or by using a wireless receiver that plugs into a USB port of the system box.

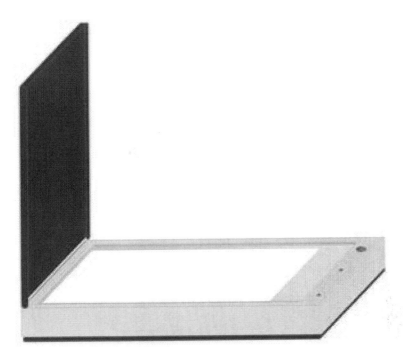

Scanner

Additional items like a printer and scanner also connect to the main system box. They connect either with a cable to the main system box or using a wireless receiver that plugs into a USB port of the system box.

Windows

Switching the power on loads the operating system (O.S). In the case of a P.C this would usually be a version of Windows. The O.S is normally loaded from the computer's hard drive.

Programs and data files are stored on the hard drive. Selecting them from the Windows Start menu starts programs.

2. Inside the P.C

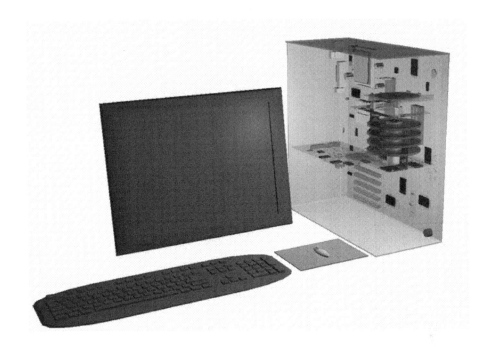

Case

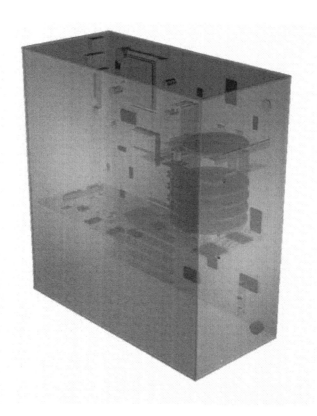

To protect the fragile P.C (personal computer) against damage it is housed in a case. Different case styles are available. A tower case is useful where desktop space is limited as it can go on the floor. The disadvantage here is accessing the CD ROM/DVD drives to change disks. A desktop case as its name implies sits underneath the monitor and allows disks to be easily accessed. The case is plastic or metal.

Peripherals

Most peripherals sit inside the case. Others for practical reasons sit outside. Often when buying additional peripherals such as a hard drive a choice is available of internal or external types.

The internal types tend to be less expensive as the casing is less protective.

Outside of the case

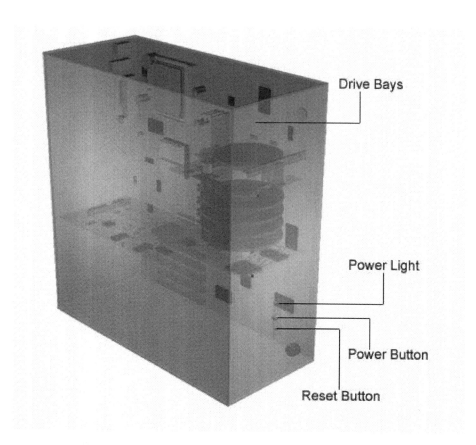

Drive Bays

Power Light

Power Button

Reset Button

On the outside of the case are the drive slots and power, reset buttons. Small l.e.ds (light emitting diodes) light up when the power is on and the hard drive is being accessed.

Connections

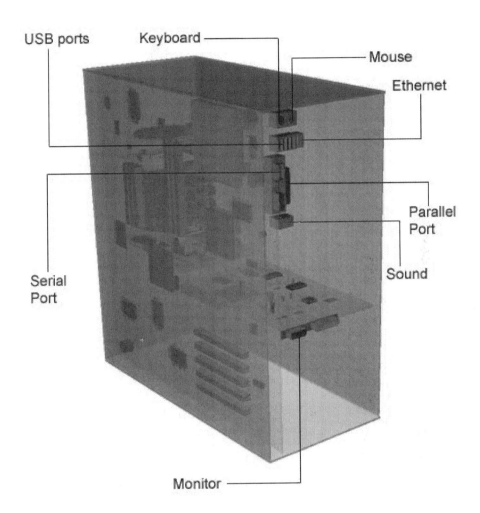

The back of the case contains all the connectors for external peripherals like the mouse, keyboard, monitor and printer.

Motherboard

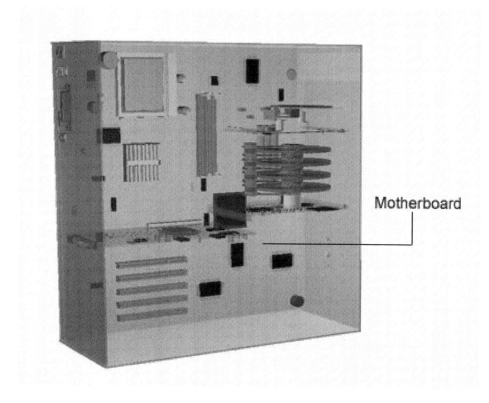

Motherboard

Inside the case a large p.c.b (printed circuit board) called the motherboard sits. The motherboard circuit and microchips control the computers operation.

E-IDE

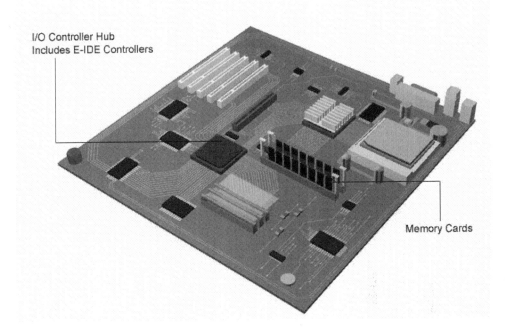

I/O Controller Hub
Includes E-IDE Controllers

Memory Cards

All internal and external peripherals connect to the motherboard. The connectors for these are soldered directly to the motherboard and protrude through the rear of the case.

Memory cards are slotted into special connector strips, this enables, where permissible, memory cards to be changed and upgraded to bigger memory cards.

E-IDE connections are made through ribbon cable to the CD-ROM/DVD and hard disks.

Jumpers

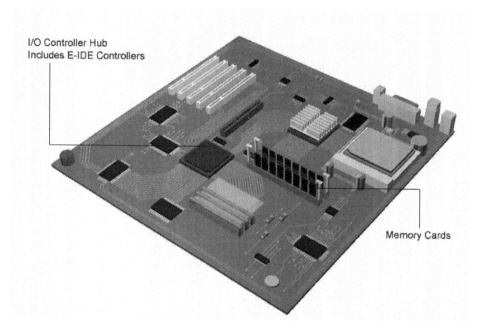

I/O Controller Hub
Includes E-IDE Controllers

Memory Cards

Spare connectors enable additional internal drives to be added. Adding a new drive is just a case of pushing a spare connector onto the drive and changing a jumper setting.

Jumper settings are small metal posts on the motherboard, which a jumper connection connects across.

Blanking Plates

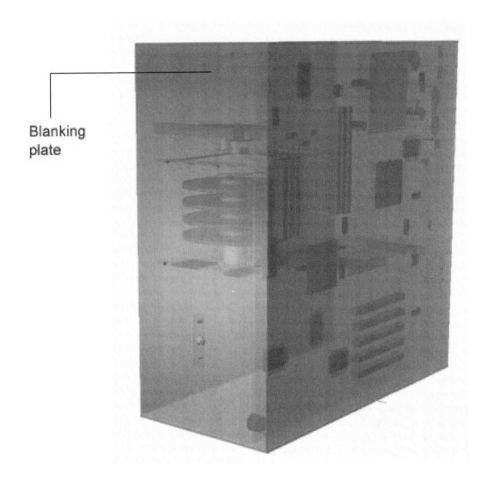

Blanking
plate

Blanking plates on the front of tower cases are pushed out for the new drive to slot in.

AGP Slot

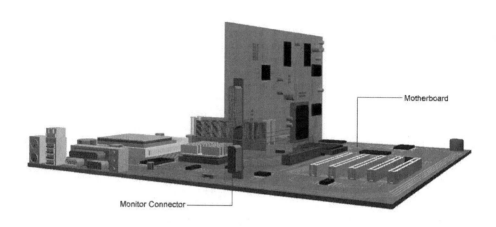

The AGP slot is where the graphics card is connected. This card interfaces the motherboard to the monitor. The monitor connector protrudes through the rear of the case.

PCI Slots

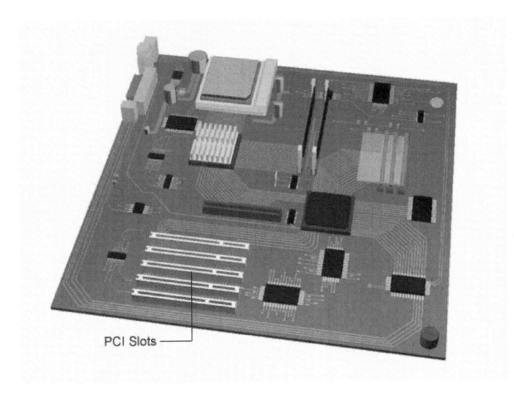

PCI Slots

 PCI slots enable expansion cards to be fitted.
Expansions cards like sound, MIDI, SCSI (small
computer systems interface).

The motherboard itself can be replaced for one with a
more powerful processor; this saves the cost of buying
a new system.

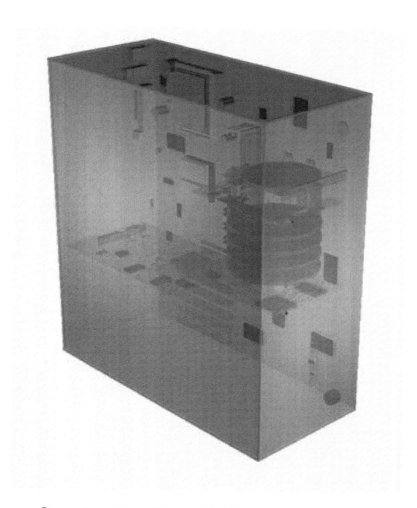

Power Supply: (Not Shown) The mains lead connects to a transformer which steps down the mains voltage to a lower voltage, 5 volts etc. Each internal component and peripheral draws their electricity from the power supply.

Case: The case is made from metal or plastic and protects all the components and peripherals from dirt and damage.

CD-ROM Drive

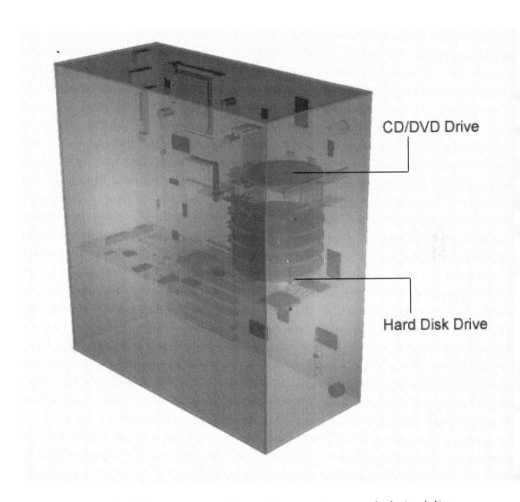

CD/DVD Drive

Hard Disk Drive

This optical drive uses a laser beam to read data bits from a CD (compact disk). Most software programs are distributed on CD.

Music CD's can also be played providing a sound card and speakers are in the system.

Most systems include a CD-RW that enables data to be written to CD-R and CD-RW disks.

A DVD drive enables DVD disks to be played in systems that have the necessary video card.

Hard Drive

Hard Drive: The operating system, programs and data files are stored on magnetic platters. The platters spin at high speed and enable data bits to be transferred to the computer at high speed.

E-IDE Controllers

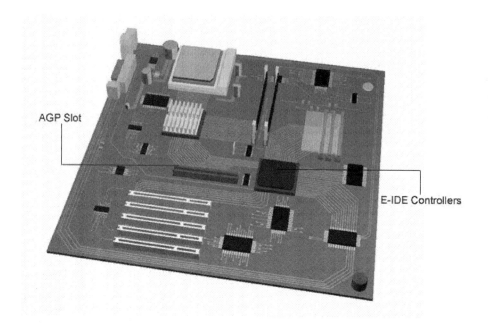

E-IDE Controllers: Built into the motherboard these provide a standard interface for transferring data bits between the drives and computer.

AGP Expansion slot: A 3D graphics card slots into the accelerated graphic port connector to provide high-speed access to the computer's memory.

Display Adapter

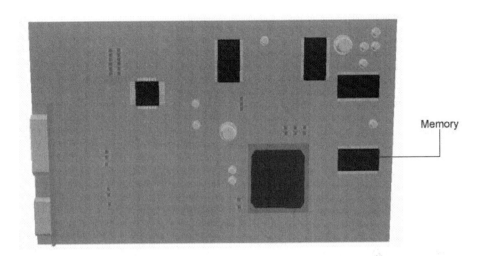

Memory

Display Adapter Interfaces the motherboard to the computers monitor. The Display Adapter (Also known as the Graphics Card) contains its own memory and microchips to display information on the monitor.

Expansion Slots

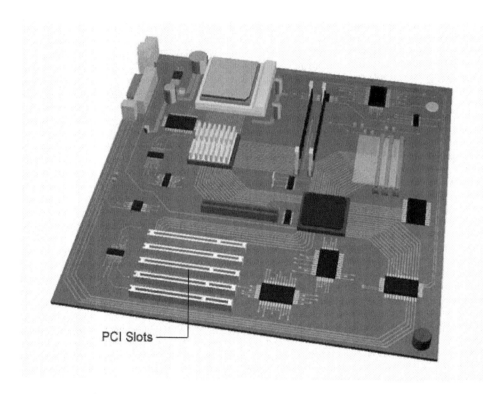

PCI Slots

PCI Expansion slot. The PCI (Peripheral component interconnect) expansion slots are designed for Plug and Play expansion cards.

Sound Card

The soundcard maybe an expansion card or be built into the motherboard. The sound card provides an analogue to digital converter (ADC) for converting external sounds into digital data bits that can be saved on the hard drive.

The card also includes a digital to analogue converter for playing sound files stored on the hard drive.

A MIDI port is also included on some cards for interfacing the computer to musical instruments.

Memory Card

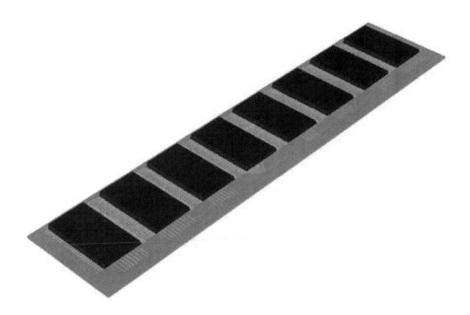

The memory card provides on-board memory for the computer.

The RAM (Random accessible memory) chips are soldered onto a small PCB that slots into a connector on the motherboard.

Clock

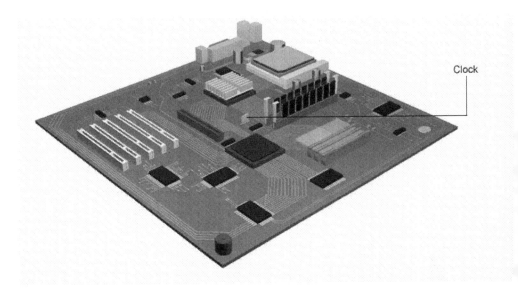

The real time clock is an electrical crystal quartz that sends out a timing signal at a certain frequency that all the microprocessors synchronize with. The clock ensures all data bits are transferred in step at the right time.

BIOS and CPU

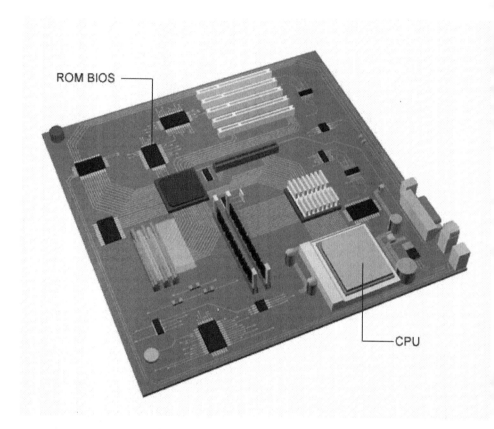

BIOS: The BIOS (basic input/output system) is an intermediary between the operating system and the various connected peripherals.

CPU: The CPU (Central Processing Unit) is the brains of the computer. Almost all data bits travel through the CPU as it carries out most of the computers operations.

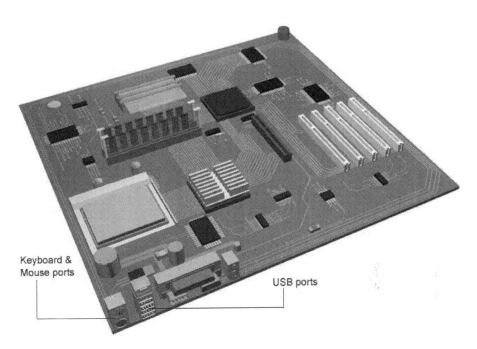

Keyboard & Mouse ports

USB ports

USB Ports: Universal serial bus ports let software programs connect directly to peripherals like the mouse, keyboard, printers and monitors without encountering resource conflicts.

Mouse Port: The mouse connects to this port, also known as a PS2 port.

Keyboard Port: The keyboard connects to this port.

Ports

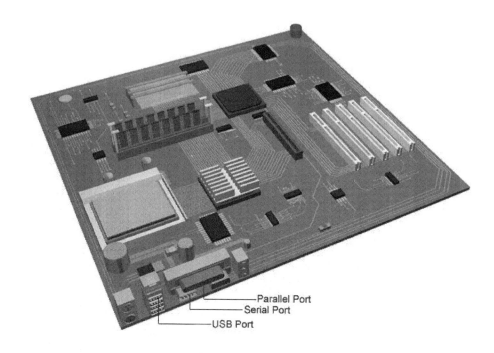

Parallel Port
Serial Port
USB Port

Parallel Port: Most often used to connect a printer.

Serial Port: The modem or certain types of mouse connect to the serial port.

3. POST

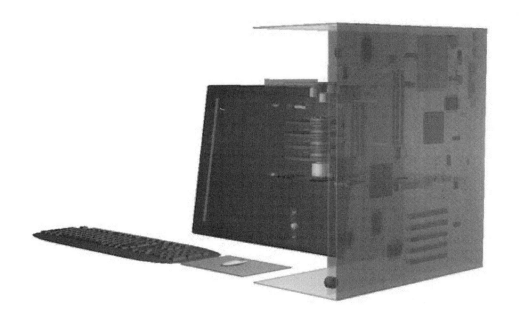

Power-On Self Test

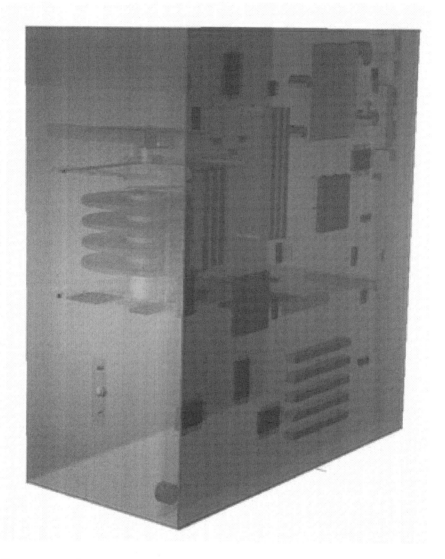

When you first switch on your PC a test is performed inside called POST (Power-On Self Test).

This operation tests your system to make sure everything is functioning before loading the operating system.

ROM BIOS

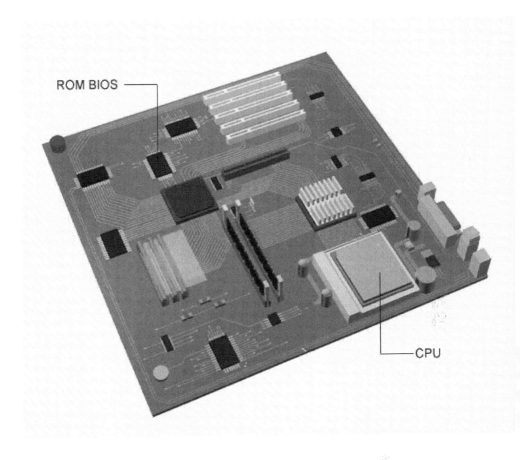

1. The test begins with a signal being sent to the CPU, which resets the internal program counter. The address for this is Hexadecimal F000. This number tells the CPU the address in the ROM BIOS which needs processing. The ROM BIOS contains at this start address a boot program that consists of a series of checks. These series of checks concern testing the CPU. Then the CPU checks the POST program by comparing the code for this in the BIOS chip.

System Bus

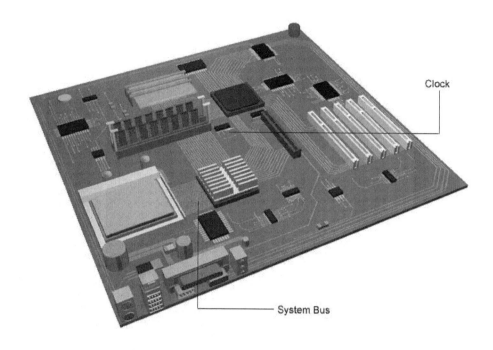

Clock

System Bus

2. The CPU sends signals over the PCI system bus to ascertain that all components are working.

3. The systems real time clock is checked by the CPU, to make sure every component is synchronized with the clock.

Display Adapter

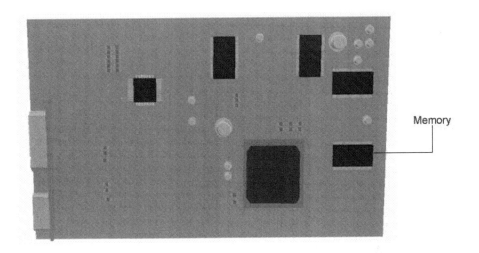

Memory

4. A test is made of the display adapters memory. The display adapters BIOS code is copied to become part of the systems BIOS.

Memory Card

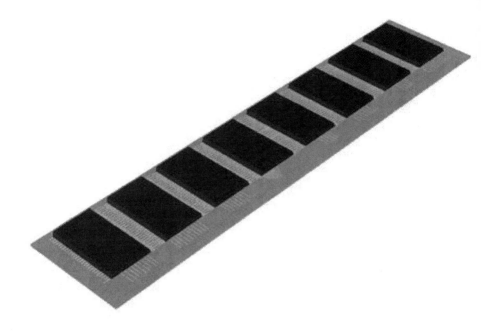

5. Depending on the type of POST your computer uses the main RAM chips on the motherboard are tested next with data written to each memory chip.

This test is not done so much with new computers with large memories as the test would take too long.

Keyboard

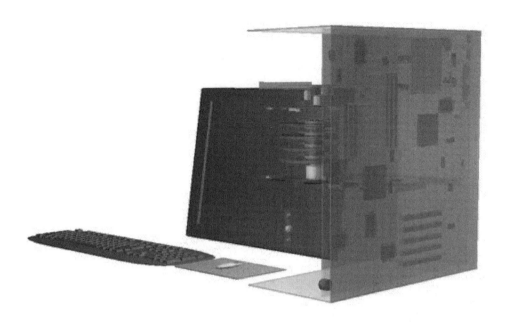

6. The keyboard is checked to make sure it's connected.

Drives

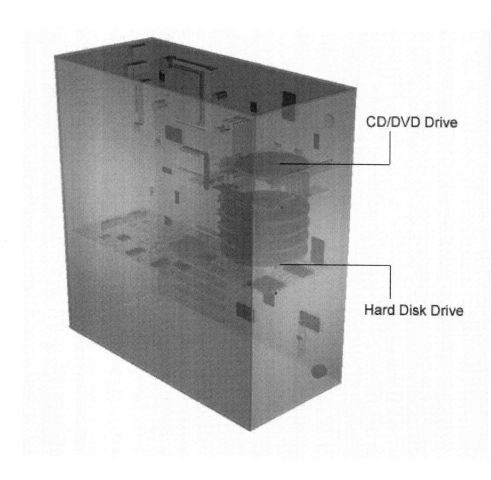

CD/DVD Drive

Hard Disk Drive

7. Next it's the turn of the floppy (if fitted) and hard drives to be tested. This check determines how many drives are available.

NV ROM BIOS

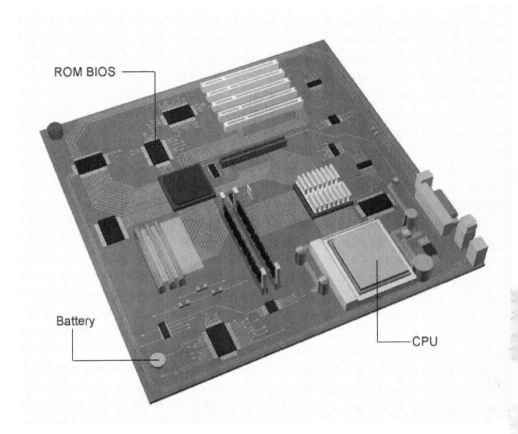

ROM BIOS

Battery

CPU

8. If these tests are successful the results are compared in the NV ROM BIOS chip. This keeps a record of which components are installed, even when the computer is switched off as a battery powers the chip. It is here, in this chip, that any changes are recorded in the system configuration.

If during the POST test new hardware is detected you can update the configuration.

SCSI Card

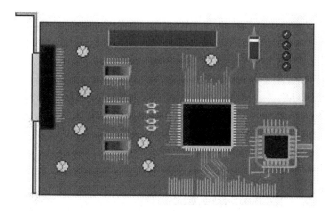

9. If a SCSI card is present its BIOS code will be transferred as with the display adapters BIOS to the main system BIOS.

With Plug and Play components and peripherals the BIOS checks each one for a unique identifier that is stored in the devices ROM.

10. The next step is to begin loading the Windows operating system.

4. BOOT UP

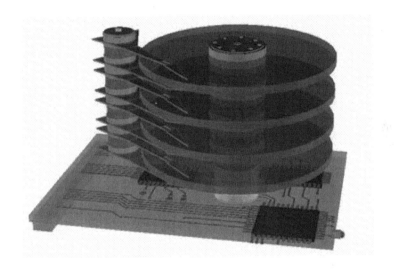

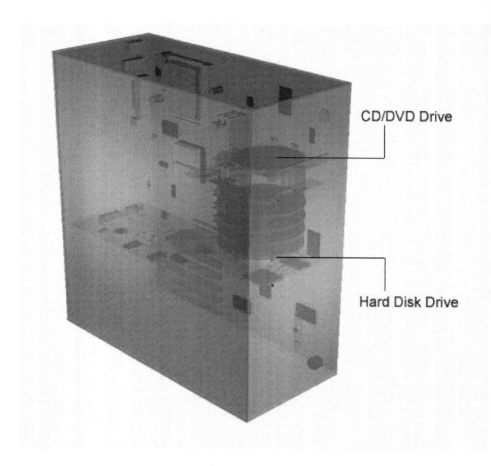

CD/DVD Drive

Hard Disk Drive

After the POST test is completed the boot program will run. The boot program is in the BIOS. On newer computers it will check the CD-ROM or DVD drive to see if a CD is present.

If a disk is present a check is made to see if two files named IO.SYS and MSDOS.SYS are present if Windows XP is being used, if they aren't an error message is generated.

Boot Record

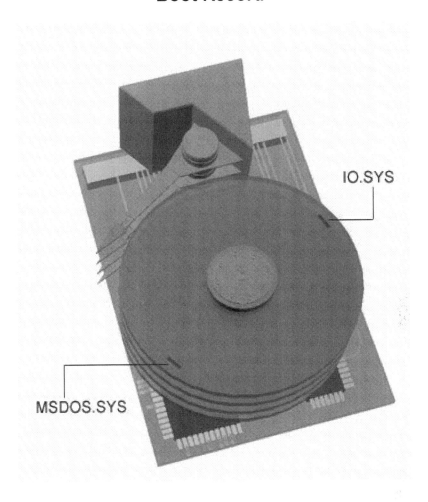

IO.SYS

MSDOS.SYS

Usually the two files reside on the hard disk so the boot program checks here next. When the two files are found both files are read into specific locations in RAM. This information is known as the boot record. The boot record is stored at the hexadecimal address 7C00. The boot record now loads the IO.SYS file into RAM.

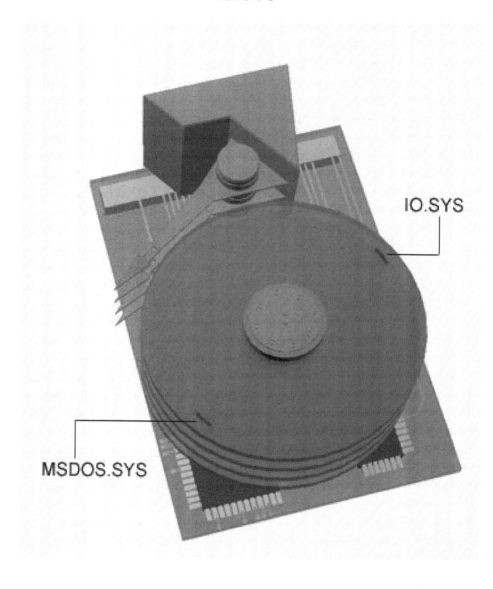

IO.SYS

MSDOS.SYS

The IO.SYS file includes a routine called SYSINIT which loads MSDOS.SYS into RAM. This file works in conjunction with the BIOS to run programs, manage files and communicate with peripherals.

CONFIG.SYS

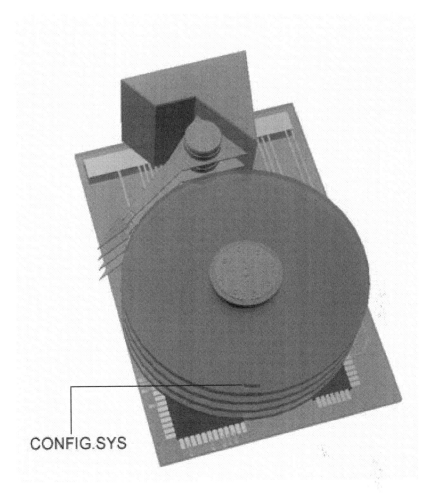

CONFIG.SYS

SYSINIT searches the root directory for the file CONFIG.SYS. MSDOS.SYS runs the commands in CONFIG.SYS. These commands inform the operating system how to perform certain operations such as how many files maybe open at one time.

Device drivers that add code to the BIOS for controlling peripherals, memory and hardware, are loaded from records in the Windows Registry file.

COMMAND.COM

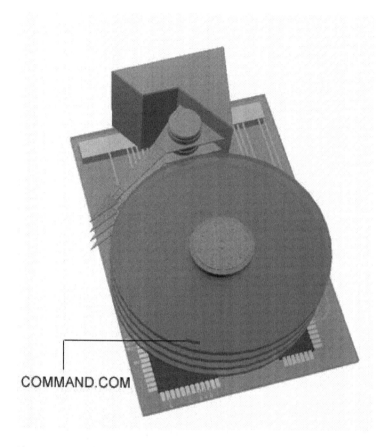

COMMAND.COM

After these actions are completed SYSINIT informs MSDOS.SYS to load the file COMMAND.COM. This file has three parts to it. Part one contains extra extensions to the input/output functions and along with the BIOS is loaded into RAM to become part of the operating system. Part two consists of the internal DOS commands like COPY, DIR. This is loaded into the high end of RAM.

AUTOEXEC.BAT

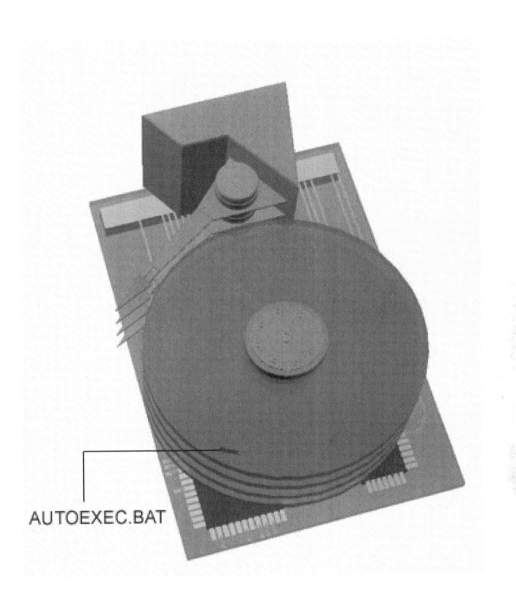

AUTOEXEC.BAT

Part three searches for a file called AUTOEXEC.BAT.
This file contains a number of DOS batch file

commands, which for instance tell the computer to load a particular program each time the computer is switched on. The boot program copies Windows, from the hard disk, to the random accessible memory RAM on the motherboard.

5. BIOS and Drivers

Save...

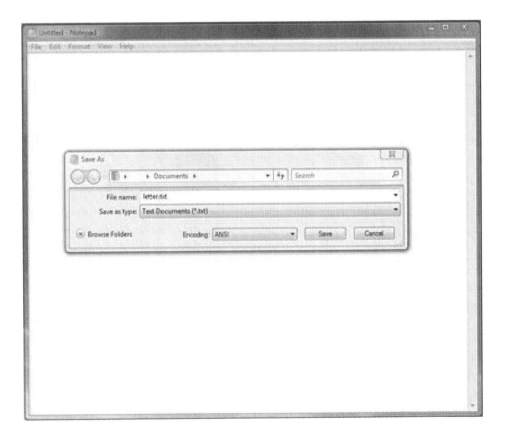

When you are running a program, like a word processor, eventually you will save a document. Selecting the Save as… option from the File menu in a word processor opens a special type of Dialog window. The save window is another example of how the o.s simplifies tasks as its operation is similar whatever program you are running. Once the save window is open and a filename entered, the o.s checks to make sure there are no problems, like the filename is valid and you're not trying to save over a read-only file.

CD ROM Drive

If there are no problems the o.s checks whether the
save function requires a device driver to control the disk
you have selected, this could be a floppy/cd drive or
hard drive. The driver contains code specific for the
drive that is selected. If the driver isn't in RAM then the
o.s copies this from the hard disk into the RAM.

Controller

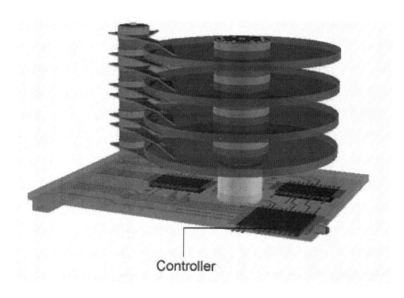

Controller

 If the selected drive has a program in the ROM BIOS, the BIOS sends the instructions and data to the drive controller. With E-IDE the controller is built into the drive if the commands are not in the BIOS it retrieves the commands from the device driver, which is written for the specific drive.

The disk controller interprets the data from the BIOS or device driver into signals, which move the read/write heads on the drive to specific locations across the media.

The drive heads create magnetic signals, which record data onto the disk's surface.

6. Plug and Play

BIOS

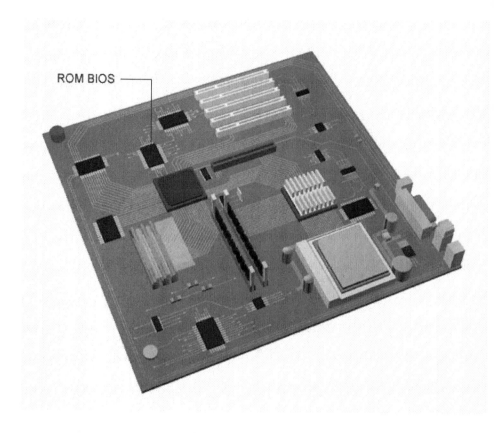

The Plug and Play standard was introduced to enable devices and peripherals to connect to the computer and work first time. When the computer is switched on. The system boots up.

The BIOS searches for all connected peripherals such as the keyboard, mouse etc.

Driver

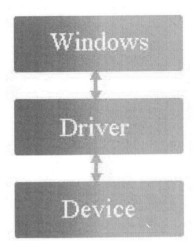

The BIOS identifies peripherals based on unique codes that are held in the peripherals ROM. After this is completed the BIOS hands over control to Windows. The Windows configuration manager adds device drivers called enumerators to itself.

Different enumerators exist for ports and SCSI. These device drivers act as an interface between Windows and different peripherals.

Windows communicates with each enumerator to establish which peripherals/devices it is going to control and what resources it requires.

Mouse: IRQ 12

Windows places this information into a database in RAM. This information is called the hardware tree. Windows examines the hardware tree for resource arbitration. Windows decides what resources i.e. interrupts (IRQs) to allocate to each peripherals/device.

Programmable Registers

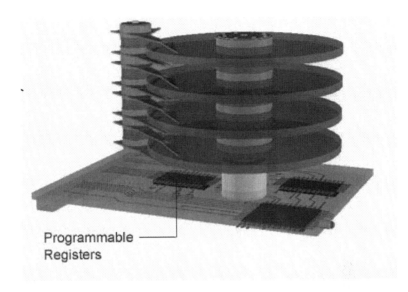

Programmable —
Registers

After this is completed the enumerators are allocated resources to their respective peripherals/device. This information is stored in the peripherals/devices programmable registers. The next stage is for Windows to search for the right device driver for each peripheral or device.

The device driver is a small program that contains information for Windows about the peripheral/device. If Windows doesn't find the right device driver it needs, it will prompt you to install it.

Loading Device Drivers

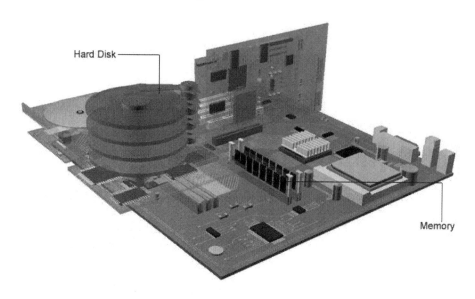

The last stage is for Windows to load all the device drivers it needs and tell each device driver what resources its device is using. The device drivers then initialise their respective peripheral /devices and Windows finishes booting up.

7. Interrupts

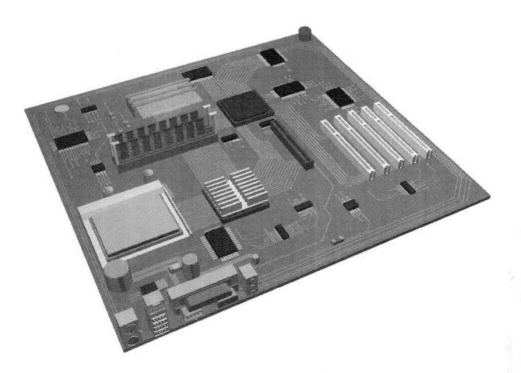

The operating system controls the input and output functions of the computer. Without an operating system every software program would have to write code for controlling the screen, keyboard, hard drive. Instead the operating system does this work for the program. By using a common interface of menus and icons you can more easily learn to use a program, without having to learn a new interface each time. Menus are in the same place and Windows look the same.

BIOS

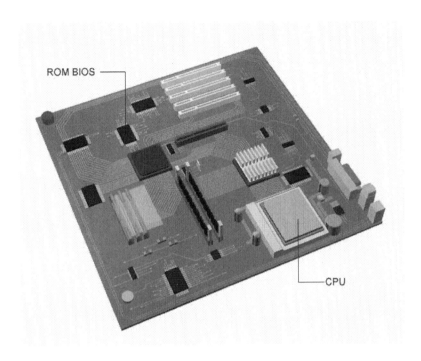

The operating system affects every data transaction on the computer. For instance it manages the type of file that can be written and the way data is sent to a printer or the way a web page is downloaded from the internet. The BIOS and device drivers interface with the operating system. Drivers interpret commands from the o.s and BIOS into instructions for peripherals like a printer or scanner. With every peripheral a specific driver is required which interfaces it to the operating system. The driver enables it to communicate with the o.s.

I/O Controller

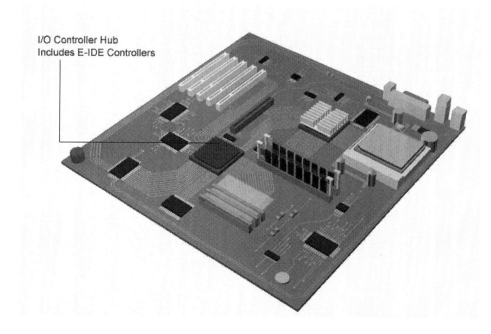

I/O Controller Hub
Includes E-IDE Controllers

When a peripheral communicates with the computer it generates a special signal known as an interrupt. An interrupt is generated every time you press a key on the keyboard or move the mouse. This signal goes to the I/O controller hub chip (ICH2).

The controller chip tells the CPU it needs to transfer data to it. The CPU in turn puts the address of the currently running program into RAM. The portion of RAM this address is stored in is called the stack.

Keyboard Interrupt

Mouse: IRQ 12

Each peripheral has an interrupt number associated with it. The IRQ number is unique to each peripheral. The CPU retrieves this number and looks in the interrupt table which is stored in RAM to find the memory address associated with a particular interrupt. The CPU reads in the instructions it found at the beginning of the address. The memory address is in the range where the BIOS was copied to during the POST test. The code is executed, if a key was pressed, code which represents the key would be sent to the program that currently has the pointers focus.

The next action is to display the character from the key on the screen. If the code instruction is completed properly the BIOS issues an IRET command, which tells the CPU to get the address of the stack in RAM, so it continues with what it was doing before the interrupt.

8. Motherboard

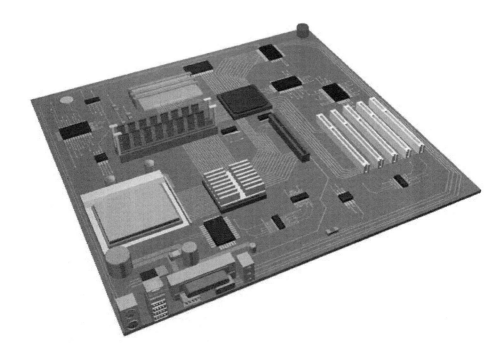

System

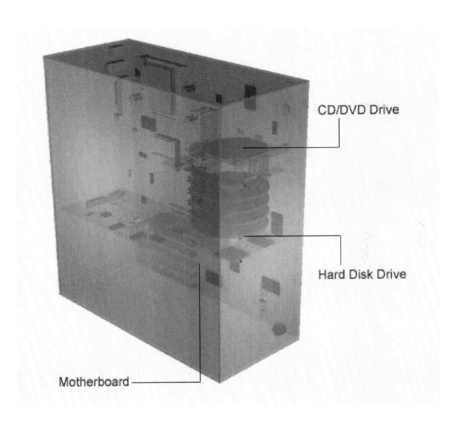

CD/DVD Drive

Hard Disk Drive

Motherboard

A computer system consists of a main case which houses the motherboard, power supply, disk and CD-ROM drives. External devices like a keyboard for typing and a mouse for opening programs and moving the on-screen pointer, connect to the motherboard.

Components

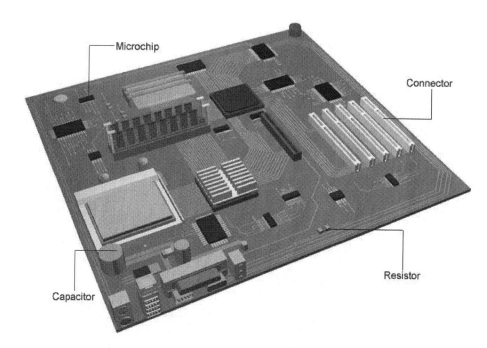

On the motherboards PCB are a number of microchips, resistors, capacitors and connectors, which are all connected into a circuit.

CPU

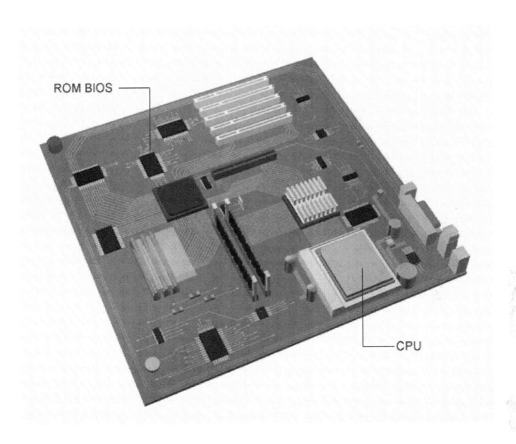

ROM BIOS

CPU

The largest microchip is the CPU (central processing unit). The CPU is the brains of the computer. Data bits are controlled and processed by the CPU.

System Bus

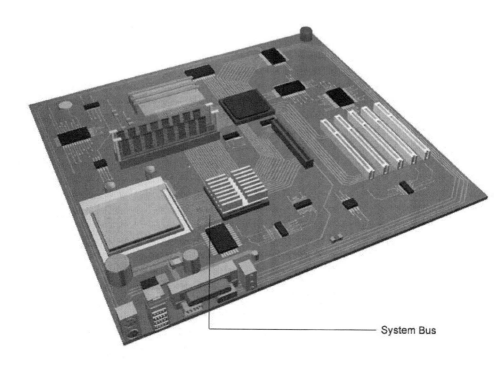

System Bus

The CPU connects directly to the system bus. The system bus is a collection of control, address and data lines.

Several local buses connect data bits to other microchips on the motherboard.

GMCH

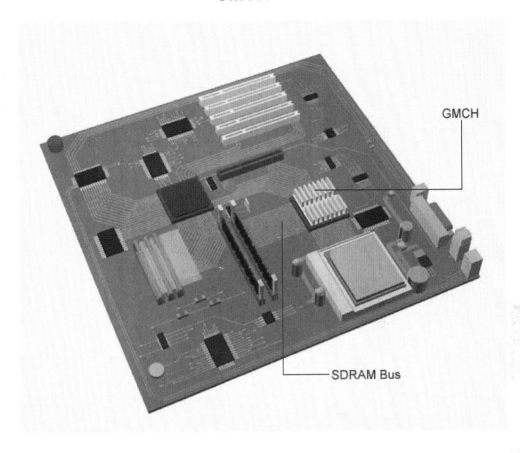

The system bus connects data bits to the graphics and memory controller hub (GMCH). The GMCH in turn places data for the memory onto the SDRAM (static dynamic random accessible memory) bus.

The SDRAM is a local bus that connects data bits to the on-board memory cards. The SDRAM bus is a collection of control, address and data lines.

AGP Connector

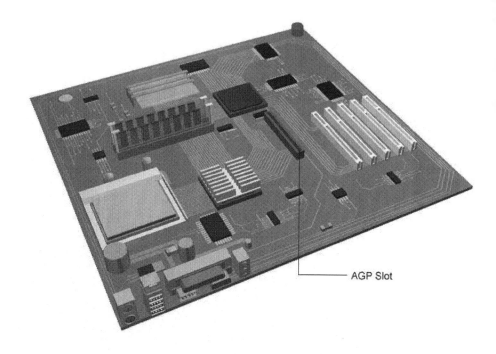

AGP Slot

The motherboard also uses the GMCH for graphics handling.

The GMCH connects separately to the AGP connector.

The AGP connector is where the graphics card for the monitor resides.

AHA Bus

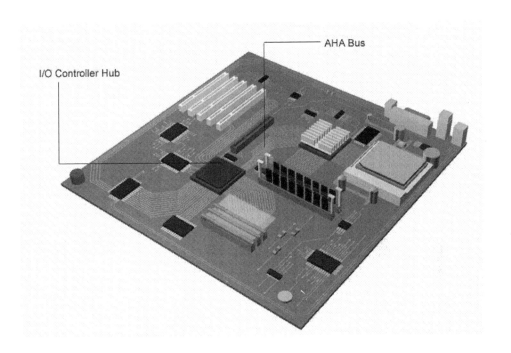

The GMCH has another local bus called the AHA bus that connects to the I/O controller hub.

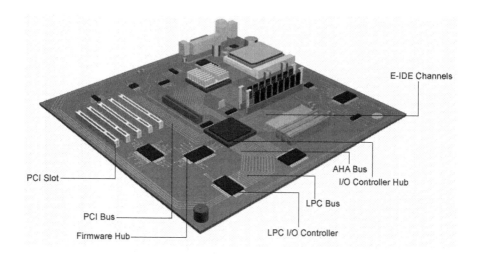

The I/O controller hub (ICH) microchip has several buses. The PCI bus connects to separate PCI slots so expansion cards can be connected to the computer.

The ICH connects to the E-IDE channels. USB ports also connect to the ICH.

The LPC bus connects to both the firmware hub (FWH) microchip (this also contains the BIOS) and LPC I/O controller.

LPC I/O

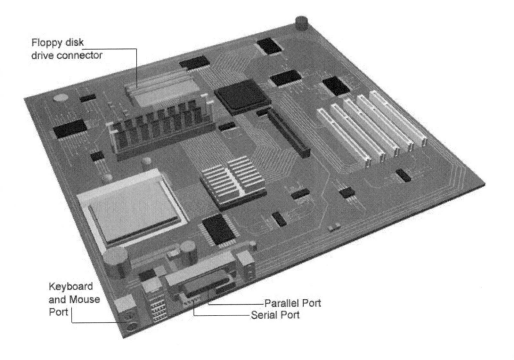

The LPC I/O connects to the floppy disk drive, two serial ports for connecting an external modem.

The parallel port, for a printer.

The mouse port, for connecting a mouse.

The keyboard port, for connecting a keyboard.

Replacing the Motherboard

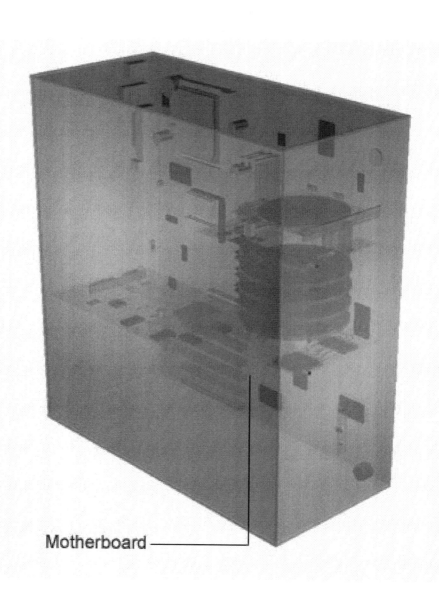

Motherboard

When your computer becomes dated it is possible to replace the motherboard for a newer higher specification one. This means you upgrade your existing machine to a higher specification at a lower cost. The CPU can often be upgraded to a faster one as it is fitted in a socket, which enables it to be changed fairly easily.

Although you will have to check whether the new CPU will run on your motherboard.

CPU

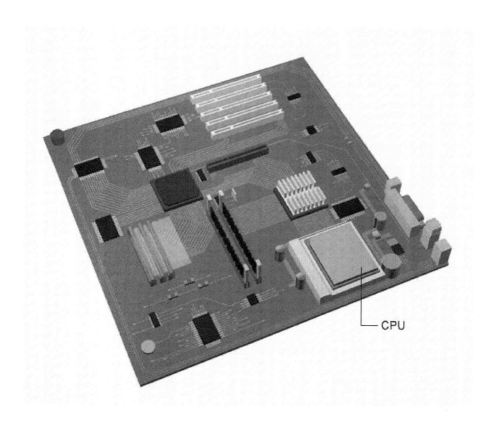

CPU

The heart of any motherboard is the CPU (central processing unit). The CPU is responsible for fetching and executing instructions, performing data calculations and placing data into memory. As the CPU can be upgraded to a higher performance version the chip is mounted in a solder less socket.

A fan sits on top to provide cooling for the chip (Not shown).

North Bridge

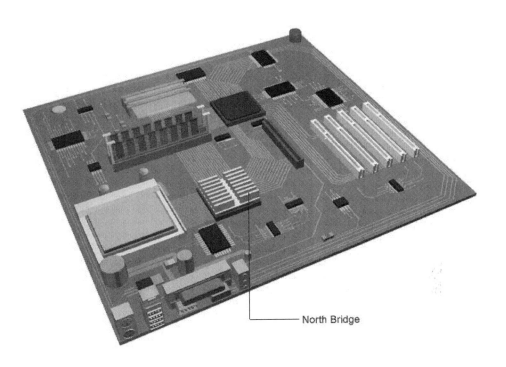

North Bridge

 The CPUs data and address lines connect it to the system bus. The bus connects to the Graphics and Memory Controller Hub (GMCH) chip, also called the "North Bridge". Some motherboards just have a memory controller in the North Bridge. This one chip controls the flow of data bits between the CPU memory, I/O and graphics card (also called the Display adapter).

Data for memory is placed on the SDRAM bus. Data for graphics is sent to the AGP/Display cache Interface. This is a connector called the AGP for a graphics card that connects to a monitor.

South Bridge

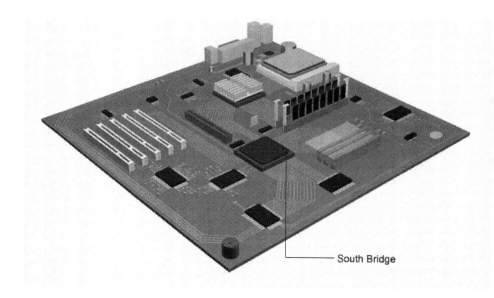

South Bridge

The GMCH chip also has another bus called the AHA bus. The AHA bus connects to the I/O controller hub, also known as the "South Bridge". The I/O controller hub controls data flow to the E-IDE channels for hard drives and CD ROMs. Up to four USB ports can be controlled.

The PCI bus connections come from the I/O controller hub to 5 edge connectors on the board. These connectors allow expansion cards to plug into the motherboard. The PCI bus connects optionally to a sound card. An optional network card may also connect to this chip.

Firmware Hub

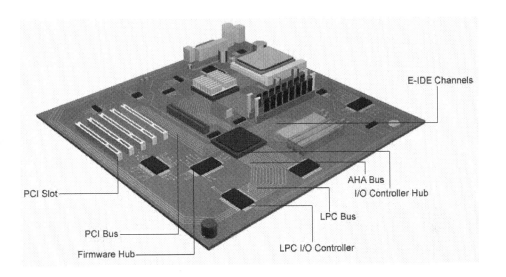

The LPC bus connects to both the Firmware hub chip and the LPC I/O controller chip. The Firmware hub chip contains the BIOS code and security features.

The LPC I/O controller connects and controls data to the disk drive two serial ports and one parallel port.

The mouse and keyboard also connect to the LPC I/O controller.

Schematic diagram of a motherboard

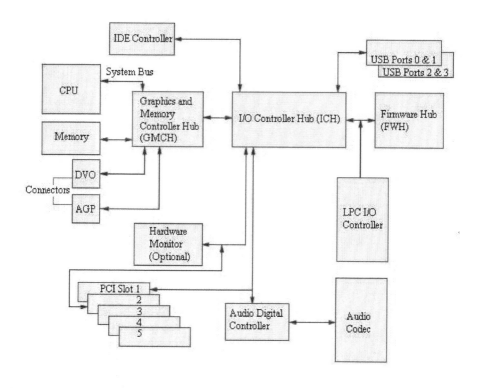

9. PCI Bus

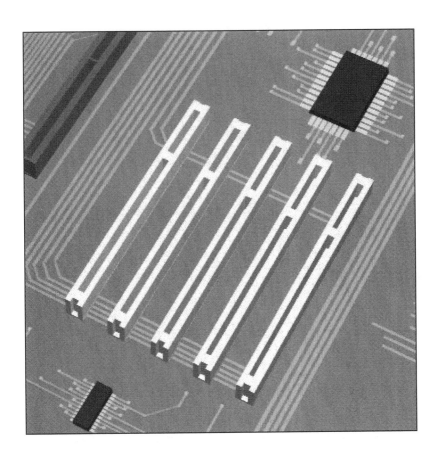

Motherboard

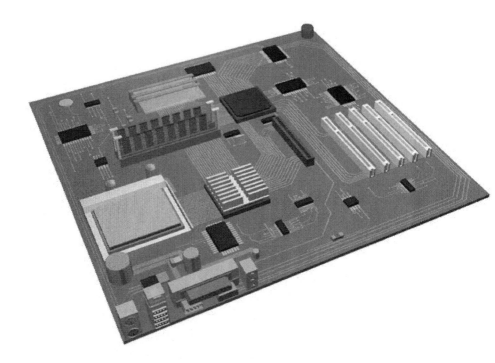

The motherboard is a large PCB fitted into the main system box. All peripherals and devices ultimately connect to the motherboard.

The motherboard contains chips for processing instructions. Connectors on the motherboard allow peripherals and devices to connect.

PCI Bus

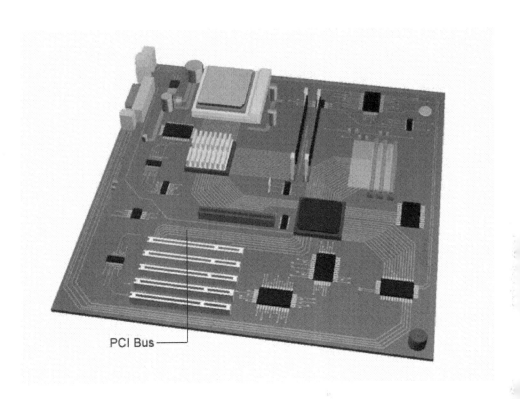

PCI Bus

Motherboards in a PC use the PCI bus specification. A system bus on a motherboard is like a 32 lane motorway where data moves between chips. The PCI bus specification exists to maintain a specification that all motherboard manufacturers can follow. This enables compatibility between computer PCs and peripherals.

Connector

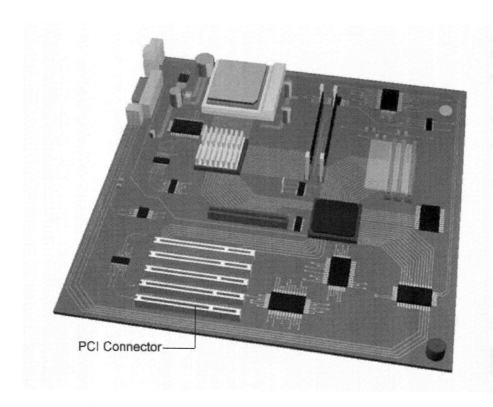

PCI Connector

Although components used on motherboards differ the specification remains consistent.

Expansion cards plug into the PCI connector. The expansion card needs to meet the PCI standard.

10. Expansion Cards

Motherboard

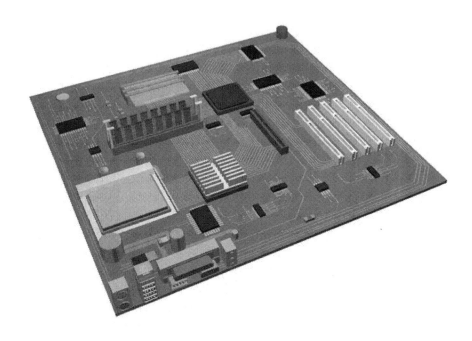

Expansion cards plug directly into the motherboard. This enables them to connect to local or system buses. Expansion cards are used for communicating with devices/ peripherals as data can be moved to them at a much higher speed than using USB ports.

PCI

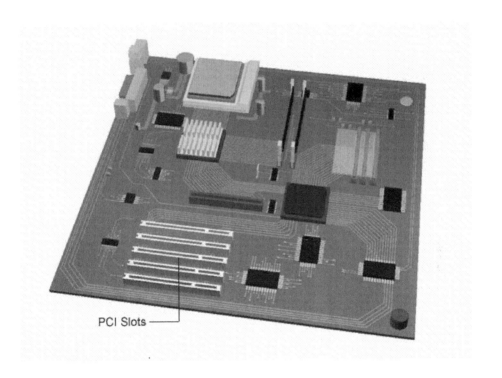

PCI Slots

Most expansion cards centre around the PCI bus standard. The 32-Bit PCI local-bus card is closely integrated with plug and play and is the most common card used in PCs.

The card handles 32 bits of data at one time.

AGP

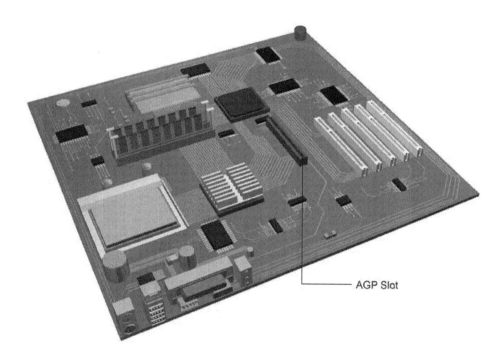

AGP Slot

An adaption of the PCI slot design is used to connect a 32-bit Accelerated Graphics Port (AGP) card. This is used to interface a monitor to the motherboard.

Graphics Card

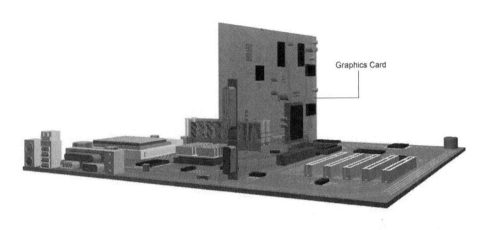

Graphics Card

The AGP is designed to accept only graphics cards as with the PCI card an edge connector that forms part of the PCB slides into a special connector on the motherboard. This connector differs from the one on the local PCI bus.

11. Serial and Parallel Ports

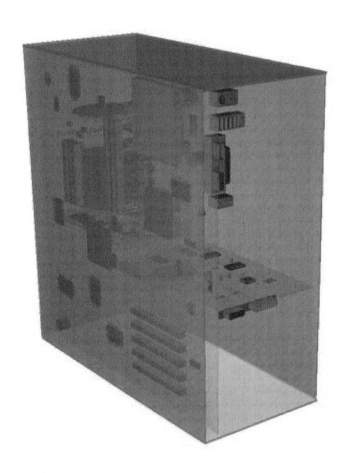

Ports

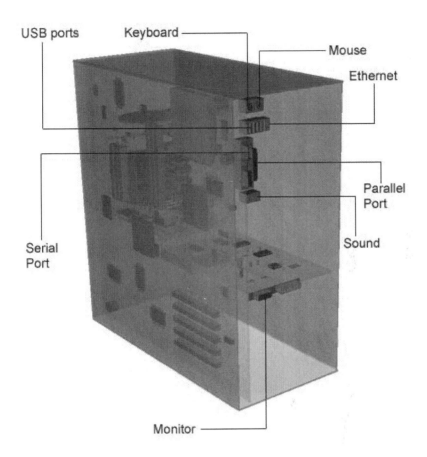

Two ports are provided on the back of the system box to connect external devices. Printers, modems, scanners connect to the ports. The serial and parallel ports are now being superseded by USB.

Serial Port

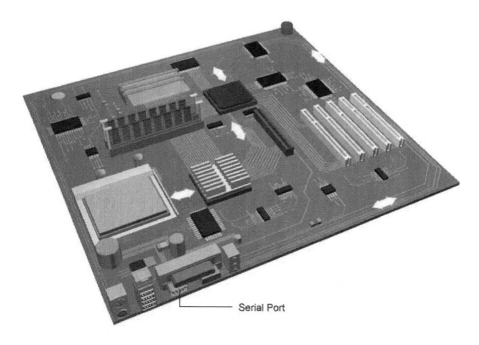

Serial Port

Data is fed to the Serial Port.

Data is fed to the I/O controller chip. Data is converted into a serial stream and connected to the serial port.

Modem

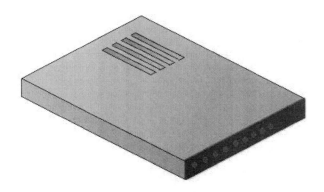

 The serial port is used typically to connect an external modem to the computer. Data bits are sent one bit after the other on one line. This is slower than the parallel port.

A 9 way D type plug on the back of the computer connects to a 25 way D connector on the modem.

Parallel Port

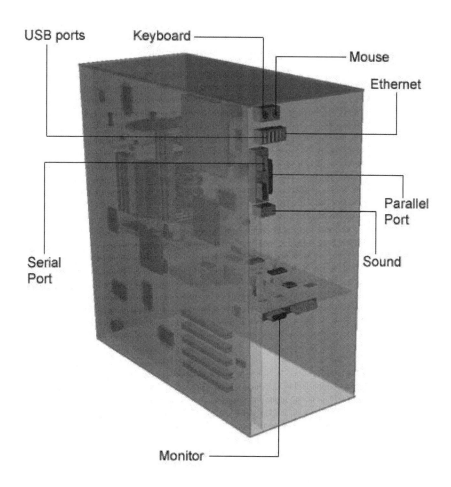

The parallel port enables data bits to travel over eight data lines to a printer The parallel port is a large D type connector on the back of the computer. A multi core cable connects this connector to a similar connector on the printer. A printer is the most often connected peripheral to the parallel port. When the printer is switched on a signal is sent to the computer. The select line signal tells the computer that the printer is online and ready to receive data. The parallel port has largely been replaced by USB for connecting printers.

Printer

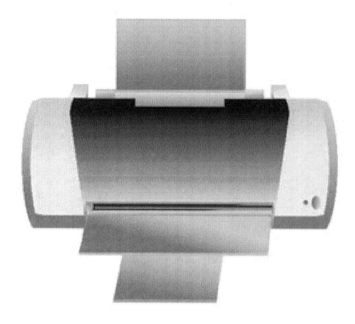

When you send a document to the printer data bits are loaded onto lines 2 to 9. Once the first data packet has been sent the computer sends a strobe signal on line 1 to the printer. This signal lasts for one microsecond and lets the printer know data is ready to be read into the printer. Once the data is read in a signal on line 10 from the printer acknowledges receiving the data sent through lines 2 to 9.

Parallel Data

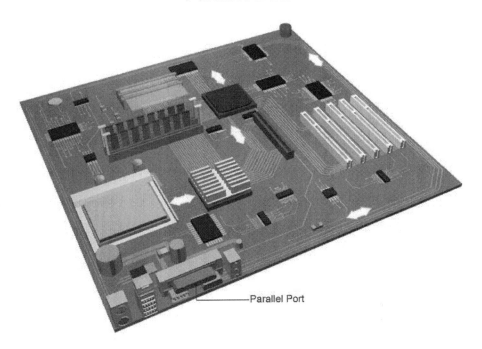

Data is fed to the Parallel port.

Line 11 from the printer tells the computer when it is too busy handling data to receive any more. When the computer receives this signal no further data is sent to the printer until the signal is cleared. Line 12 sends a signal to the computer when the printer runs out of paper. Line 15 is a general error line used by the printer to tell the computer an error has occurred such as jammed paper etc. Line 16 is a signal from the computer that resets the printer to its original power up state.

12. CPU

Central Processing Unit

The central processing unit (CPU) is the heart of any computer. The CPU performs many tasks on data. Most data at one stage will travel through the CPU.

The CPU performs calculations on data, routes data to memory and organizes data. The chances are your computer will contain a CPU from either Intel or AMD.

Intel's Pentium processors are amongst the most widely used.

Different CPU speeds are available, the higher speed CPU's process data much faster, so the computer will perform tasks faster.

Clock

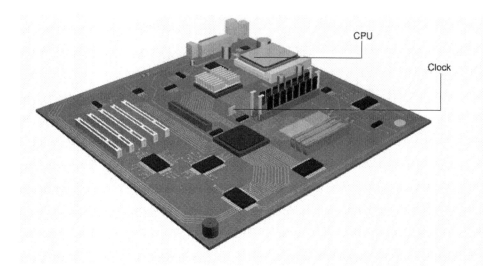

The CPU is attached to the motherboard. A quartz crystal clock generates timing pulses that are fed into the CPU and other microchips. These timing pulses keep the CPU data processing in step with all the other microchips on the motherboard. Because of the huge amount of heat generated by the CPU, a fan (not shown) keeps it cool.

Intel Pentium

Here we describe the internal operation of an Intel Pentium processor.

The Intel Pentium CPU microprocessor uses millions of transistors on its two silicon circuits.

One circuit is the main CPU. A memory cache, named L2 is the second. Both silicon circuits are embedded in the one package with connection leads underneath.

The CPU and memory cache are 64bits wide. Data bits move around the Pentium up to 100Mhz.

Each data bits movement is controlled by a clock pulse so all movements happen at the same time.

The timing cycle ensures data moves around at the same speed.

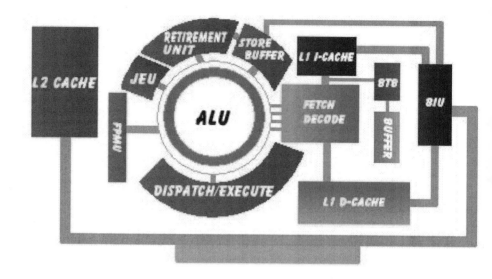

Internal Pentium Diagram

BIU

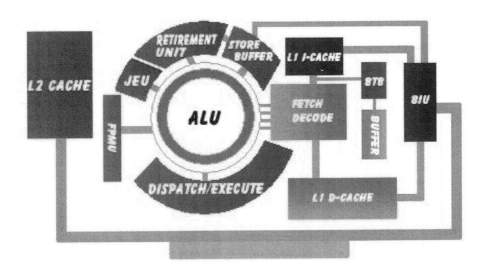

Idle

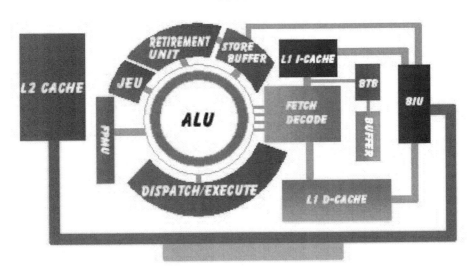

Data is read into the BIU and placed in the L2 cache

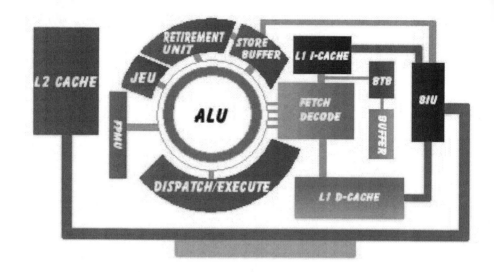

BIU copies data to L1 caches

When data bits reach the CPU data is connected to the CPUs bus interface unit (BIU). Once the BIU receives information it makes a copy of it.

One copy is sent to the L2 memory cache the other to L1 memory caches on the main CPU silicon circuit.

There are several L1 memory caches on the main CPUs silicon circuit and range in size from 8-16KB.

The BIU sends code to the L1 instruction cache, or I-cache. Data is sent to the Data cache (D-cache) to be used by the code.

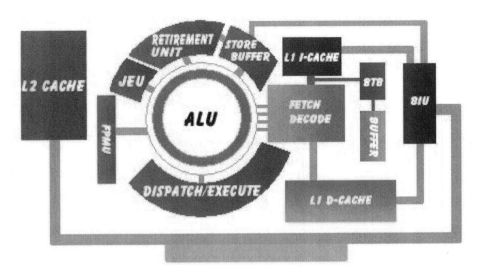

The Fetch/Decode Unit pulls data from the L1 I-Cache the BTB also has this data

The fetch/decode unit pulls instruction code from the I-cache, at this time the branch target buffer (BTB) compares each instruction code with a record in a separate memory buffer to see if it's been used before.

The BTB is searching for any code which involves branching. This is because the program code could follow separate paths.

If the BTB finds a branch type instruction it predicts where the program will go. The BTB does this from past experience; its predications are over 90 percent accurate.

Reorder Buffer (ROB)

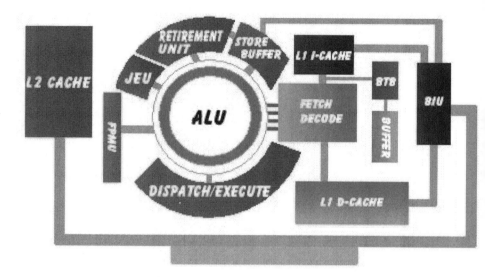

Data is sent to the ROB

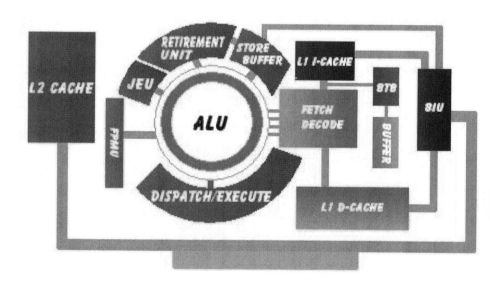

The Dispatch/Execute unit checks and executes code

Three decoders working in parallel break up the larger instructions into uops (mu-ops) these are smaller 274 bit micro-operations.

The dispatch/execute unit processes a uops faster than a single higher-level instruction code.

The decode unit sends all uops to the Reorder Buffer (ROB) also called the instruction pool. The Reorder Buffer contains two arithmetic logic units (ALUs).

The ALUs handle all integer number calculations and contain the uops in the order the BTB predicted.

Dispatch/Execute

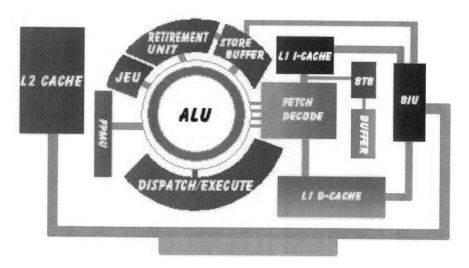

The ALUs use a circular buffer with a head and tail to mark the beginning and end of the uops lines. From here the dispatch/execute unit checks in the buffer each uop to see whether all the information is there to process it.

If the code is valid the dispatch/execute unit carries out the code. When a uop requires data bits from memory, the execute unit skips over it.

The CPU looks for the information in the L1 memory cache. If the data bits are not there the L2 memory cache is checked.

Memory Cache

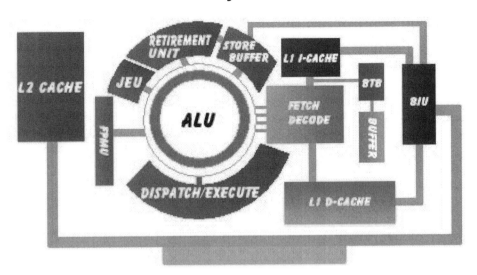

If neither memory cache holds the data bits they are retrieved from the main on board memory. Going to the on-board memory slows down data processing, as retrieving data from the on chip caches is much faster than going to on-board memory.

While data bits are being fetched from memory the execute unit continues inspecting each uop in the buffer.

When a valid micro-op has all the required information the unit processes it and stores the results in the uop itself.

The code is then marked as complete.

Floating-Point Math Unit

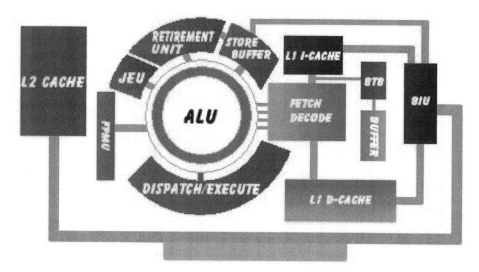

The Dispatch/Execute unit checks and executes code

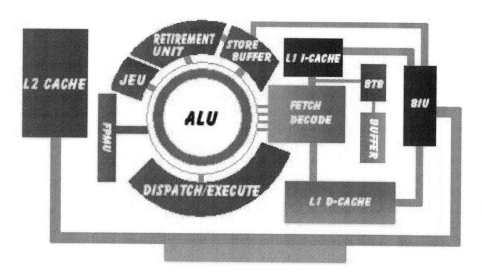

The floating point maths unit (FPMU) performs calculations

The execute unit moves onto the next uop in line. This method of processing is called speculative execution as the order of uops in the circular buffer is based on the BTB's branch predictions.

When the end of the buffer is reached, the execution unit starts at the beginning (head) again and checks all the uops to see whether any have received data bits that need to be executed. During instruction processing if a floating-point number is found the ALU's pass this to the floating-point math unit that contains circuits that are optimised to process floating point numbers quickly.

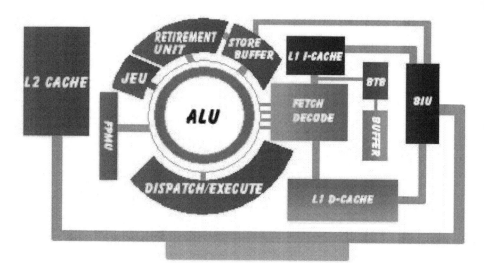

The JEU unit in action

Delayed uop instructions are processed and the execute unit compares the results with those predicted by the BTB.

If a prediction comparison is wrong the jump execution unit (JEU) moves the end marker from the last uop in line to the predicted uop.

All uops behind the end marker can be ignored and overwritten by new uops.

Retirement Unit

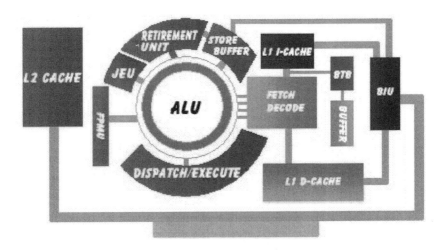

Data is sent to the retirement unit

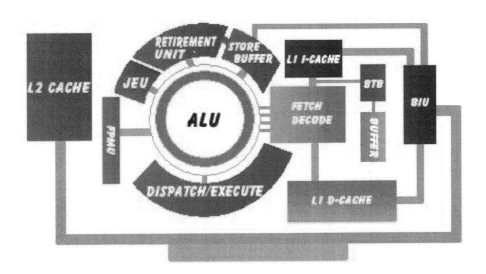

The retirement unit sends data to the store buffer

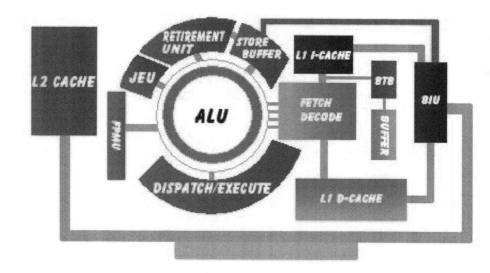

The completed data is sent back to the BIU

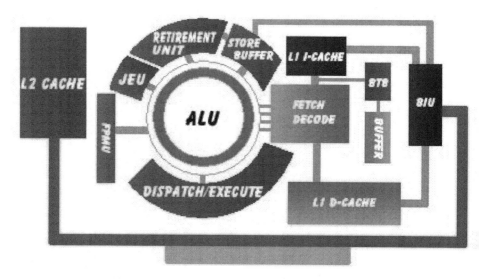

Data is placed onto the CPUs system bus

The BTB is informed that its prediction was wrong, and that information becomes part of its future predications. During these processes the retirement unit checks the circular buffer to see whether the head uop has been carried out.

In the case it hasn't, the retirement unit keeps checking until it has. The retirement unit checks the second and third uops.

If they have also been executed all three results are sent to the store buffer.

When they arrive here the retirement unit checks them again before they are sent to the main on board memory.

13. PCB

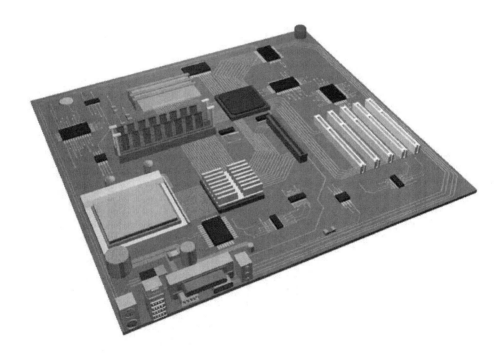

Printed Circuit Board

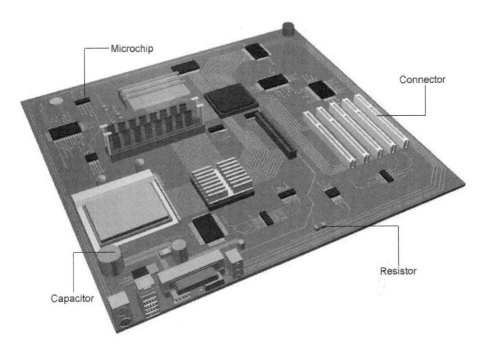

The printed circuit board (PCB) contains components such as microchips, resistors, capacitors and connectors for plugging in peripherals.

The motherboard is the largest circuit board in the computer.

Multilayer

Circuit boards have arrays of copper tracks on each side of the board. Extra boards can be glued together to form a multilayer circuit board.

An extra board is used when connection lines would otherwise cross and short out on other connections.

Socket

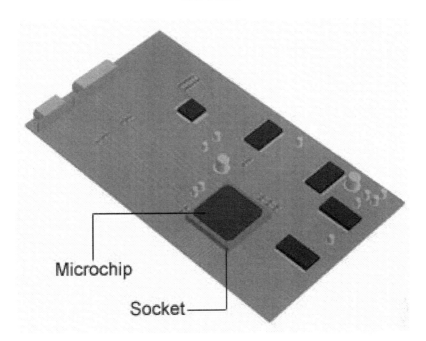

Microchip

Socket

 All components are soldered to the copper tracks on the circuit board. Where components may need replacing in the future like the CPU, sockets are used where the microchip can be replaced easily.

This makes upgrading the computers processor easy as un-soldering lots of solder joints would probably ruin the circuit board.

The substrate of the board is usually glass fibre with the tracks etched onto the board.

14. Memory

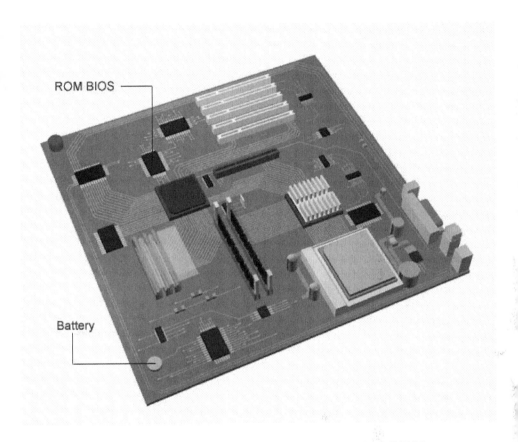

ROM BIOS

Battery

Memory chips retain and store data from the CPU. Data is held in the memory while power is on. Once the computer is switched off data is lost. Some types of memory chips like the ROM BIOS retain their data with a battery.

These memory chips are called non-volatile types as they retain their data even when the computer is switched off.

DRAM, EDO RAM, SRAM

These are the commonest forms of memory chips. DRAM (Dynamic random access memory). This is most likely to be in your computer.

Dynamic means the storage capacitors in the chip have to be refreshed every thousandth of a second or data will be lost. EDO RAM (Extended Data out random access memory).

This type of memory can send data out while receiving another address so making it faster than DRAM.

SRAM (Static random access memory) SRAM is usually faster than DRAM as it doesn't need to be refreshed, but is more expensive.

VRAM

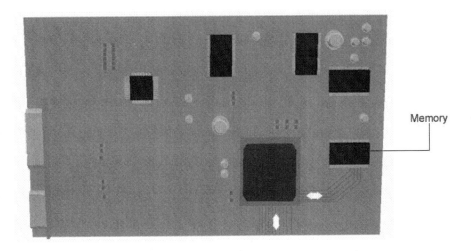

Memory

Data being read into Memory (VRAM)

 VRAM (Video random access memory) Found on the display adapter VRAM chips include two ports so data can be written into memory while the card reads the address locations to refresh the screen.

SIMM, DIMM,ECC

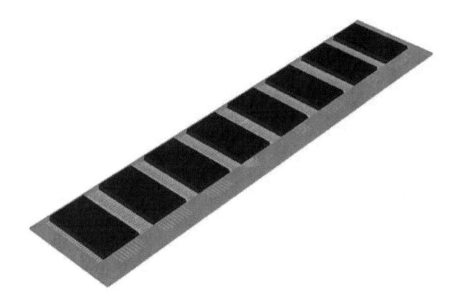

SIMM (single in-line memory modules) Memory chips are mounted on a small PCB with connecting pins on one edge that plug into a special socket on the motherboard.

DIMM (Dual in-line memory module) Similar to SIMMs but have memory on both sides of the circuit board. ECC (Error-correcting code) Memory that uses extra data bits to check for errors.

Connections

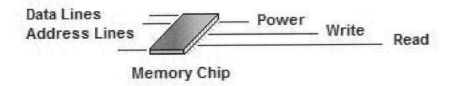

Memory Chip

There are four main types of connections to memory chips. One provides power to the chip. Several connections are required for read and write operations.

Most data bit lines are associated with sending an address, which reads or writes data from a specific location in the memory chip.

Address and Data Lines

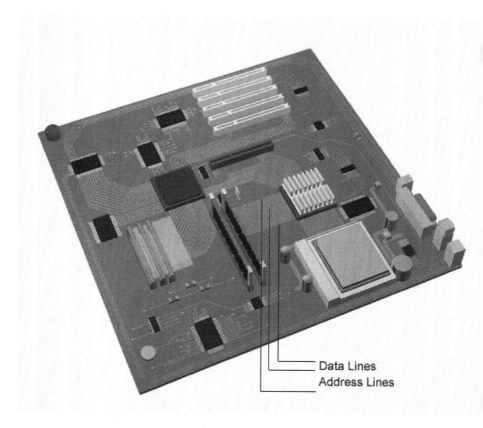

Data Lines
Address Lines

Typically a memory chip has many address and data lines. The address is made up of parallel data bits travelling to a group of memory chips. With this address "1010110010101100" each bit travels to the memory board along its own dedicated line.

When the CPU along the system bus sends the address, the CPU also sends the actual data bits it wishes to store in the memory. These data bits are stored in memory at a position pointed to by the address.

Access Time

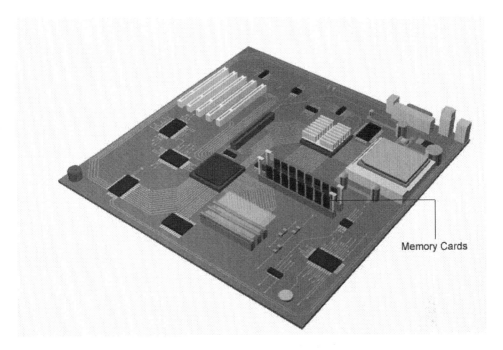

Memory Cards

The number of locations in memory, where data bits can be stored, is governed by the number of different address number combinations that can be made with a binary number. When reading from memory the access time of the memory chip is important.

The access time (measured in nanoseconds) is the total time the memory chip takes to internally retrieve data.

If the memory chip is slow then overall time for performing tasks with the CPU will increase. The main memory RAM is contained on the motherboard in DIMM (Dual in-line Memory Modules).

CPU

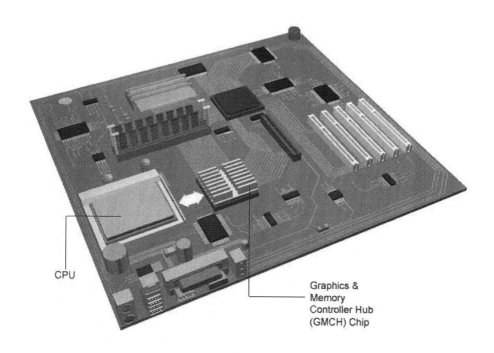

CPU

Graphics &
Memory
Controller Hub
(GMCH) Chip

Data is transferred from the CPU to the GMCH Controller

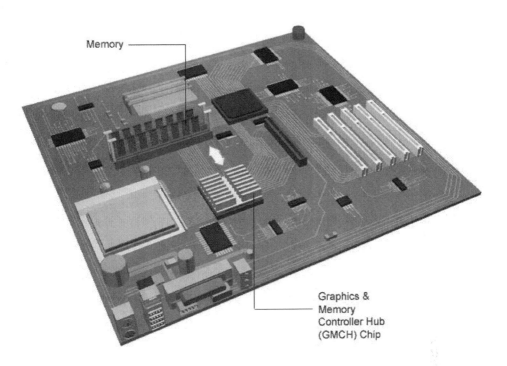

Memory

Graphics &
Memory
Controller Hub
(GMCH) Chip

GMCH Controller sends address to Memory

The CPU issues data and a memory address for the data to be stored at. These two are placed on the system bus that connects to the Graphics and memory controller hub chip (GMCH).

The data is placed onto the SDRAM bus and routed to the main system memory RAM. Once inside the memory chips data is stored at that specific address.

Graphics and Memory Controller hub

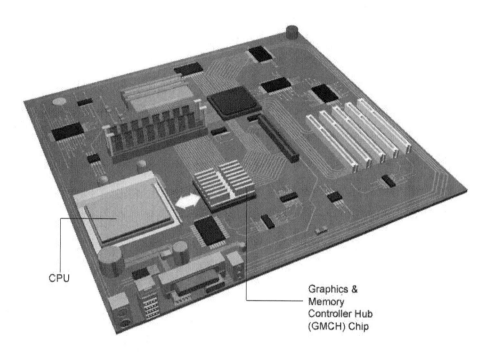

CPU

Graphics &
Memory
Controller Hub
(GMCH) Chip

Address is transferred from the CPU to the GMCH Controller

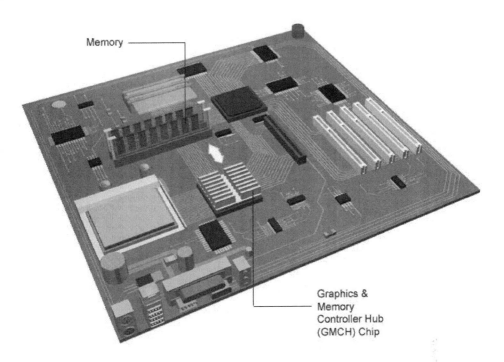

Memory

Graphics &
Memory
Controller Hub
(GMCH) Chip

GMCH Controller sends address to Memory

When the CPU wishes to retrieve data from memory it issues an address that is placed on the system bus that connects to the Graphics and memory controller hub chip.

The address is routed to the main system memory RAM. Depending on the access time of the chip (measured in nanoseconds) the data is retrieved and placed on the SDRAM bus which connects the memory to the Graphics and memory controller hub chip.

The data is then placed on the system bus ready to be read in by the CPU.

Silicon Circuit

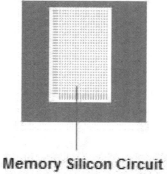

Memory Silicon Circuit

Inside the memory chip are thousands of transistors and capacitors etched onto a silicon circuit.

15. Mouse

Introduction

Pointer

The mouse is designed to move the on-screen pointer. Moving the screen pointer is intuitive as it moves in-relation to the movements of the mouse. The mouse as a pointing device comes into its own, as it is quick and easy to use. Inside the mouse is a rubber ball, this protrudes slightly from the base.

The ball rotates when in contact with a flat surface such as a mat. These movements are translated into positions which the on-screen pointer moves to.

Mouse Switches

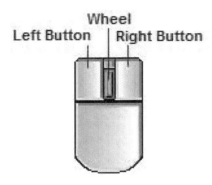

The switches on top enable programs to be run and menu items selected. Pressing the left mouse button enables applications to be launched when the pointer is over a desktop icon or menu item. The right mouse button opens menus. The wheel allows scrolling up or down, left or right. To activate this feature you need to press the wheel down once.

Inside the Mouse

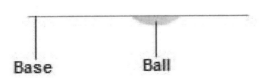

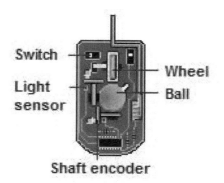

Switch

Light sensor

Wheel

Ball

Shaft encoder

Protruding from underneath the mouse is part of a rubber ball. The ball rotates when in contact with a surface. Inside the mouse the grey cylindrical ball is in contact with two shafts, one shaft rotates when the mouse moves up or down the other when the mouse moves left or right.

In addition both shafts rotate when for instance the mouse is moved at an angle of 265 degrees.

Shaft Encoders

Each shaft has a perforated disk on one end, known as an encoder. A tiny light shines through a small perforation around the edge each time the shaft rotates. As the mouse moves, the ball rotates and each shaft turns.

Each time the shaft rotates a perforation in the end disk lets light through, which is picked up by a light sensor. When the light sensor detects light, a low voltage is produced.

The light sensor is connected to a chip. This happens each time the mouse is moved. When the mouse is moving quickly this process is repeated many times. The signal goes along the cable to the computer.

Mouse Movements

Horizontal Movement

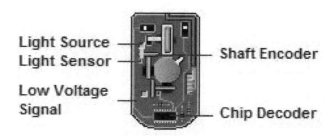

Light Source
Light Sensor

Low Voltage
Signal

Shaft Encoder

Chip Decoder

Vertical Movement

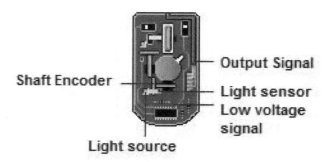

Shaft Encoder

Output Signal

Light sensor
Low voltage
signal

Light source

These two diagrams show what happens each time you move the mouse.

The Mouse and Motherboard

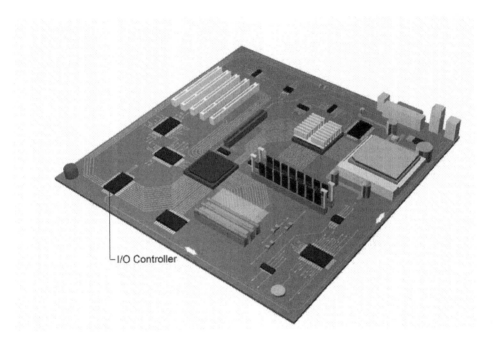

I/O Controller

Mouse movement is transferred to I/O Controller from mouse port.

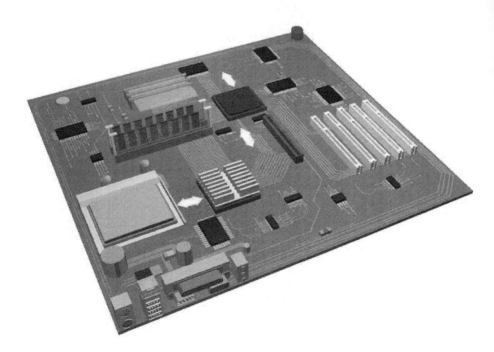

Inside the computer the I/O controller reads in the mouse signals and Windows converts these signals into a current position for the on-screen pointer.

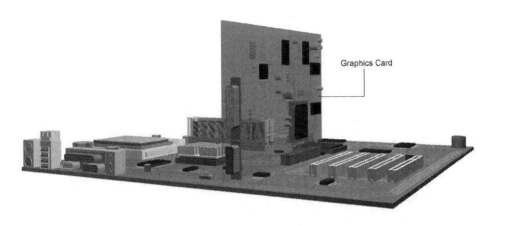

Graphics Card

The graphics card (also known as the display adapter) VRAM is updated as moving the pointer changes the screen. This is updated to reflect the pointers new position.

This sequence of events takes place every time you move the mouse.

16. Keyboard

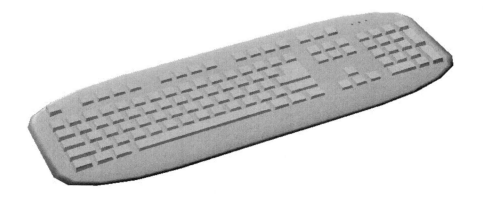

Introduction

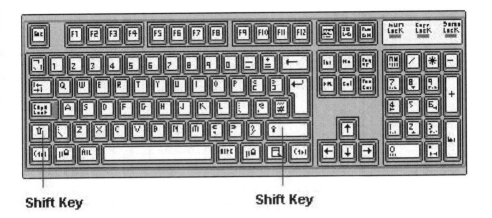

Shift Key   Shift Key

The keyboard is the main input device we use to communicate with the computer. The keyboards purpose is to pass numbers, letters and special function keys to the computer. These are passed when a specific key is pressed. Using a combination of keys enables certain keys to have dual functions.

For instance when the Shift key is down letter keys become CAPITAL LETTERS instead of lower case letters. This is useful as it cuts down on the number of keys required. Imagine the size of keyboard required if this was not the case.

Keyboard

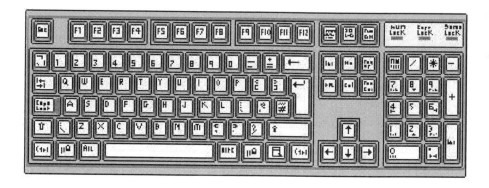

The keys on the keyboard are individual switches. When a key is pressed a special code is sent to the computer. The computers BIOS chip recognises the code and interprets this into a number or letter. The keyboard layout has not really changed since the days of the original typewriter.

Keyboards are known as QWERTY keyboards as they represent the first six letters. The keyboard above is a 104-key Windows version.

Keys

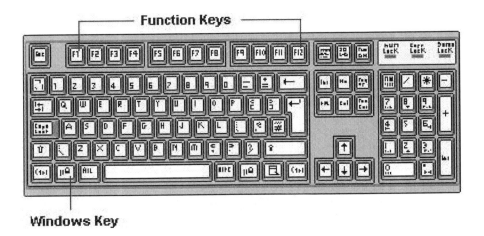

This keyboard has keys, which offer functions, which are used in conjunction with the Windows operating system. For instance the key on the bottom row two in from the left opens the Start menu. The top row consists of twelve function keys labelled F1 to F12. These keys are used by certain software packages to carry out tasks.

A good example is Word, which uses the F7 key to start spell checking. Another piece of software may use F7 to carry out another task so the function of the key changes with the software you are using. You may find the key isn't used at all in a program.

Numeric Keypad

Numeric Keypad

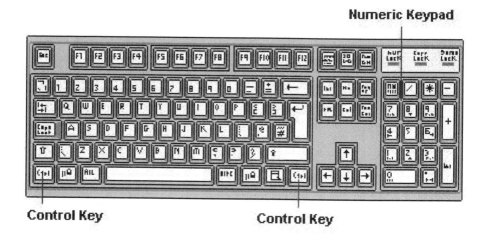

Control Key   Control Key

 On the right hand side are a group of keys known as the Numeric keypad. These keys are useful as their layout enables quicker data entry of numbers than would be possible using the number row above the letter keys. The bottom left hand key is the Control key labelled Ctrl.

This key when used with other keys enables for example menu options to be used without opening them with the mouse.

Key Functions

Tab Key   Delete Key   Page Down Key

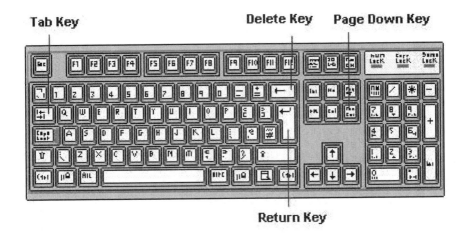

Return Key

Holding down the Control key and f key in Word opens the Find and Replace dialog window. Other keys, which have non-writing functions are, the Page Up and Page Down keys, which in Word scroll the screen up or down a page. The arrow keys enable the cursor to move up through lines in Word. The Return key is used to start a new line in Word.

The Delete key deletes the last letter/number typed in. The Tab key creates fixed spaces between letters/numbers which is useful for creating presentations.

Inside a Key

Grid Matrixs

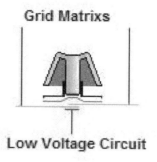

Low Voltage Circuit

**When the key is down
the grid matrixs connect
to the low voltage**

In a typical keyboard the key switch sits above a special plastic circuit board. When the key is pressed it pushes onto a rubber dome which in turn compresses three circuit connections together. The bottom circuit contains low voltage electricity. This passes through to the other two circuits, but only when the key is pressed down.

Keyboard Matrix

Key switch pads   Matrix Line   Decoder chip

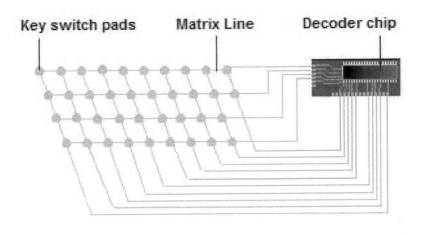

 Inside the keyboard a matrix of conducting circuits interconnect each of the keys to a decoder chip. Once a key is pressed the rubber dome represented by a circle here presses the two matrix connections together.

The decoder chip senses which key has been pressed and sends a hexadecimal code to the computer.

I/O Controller

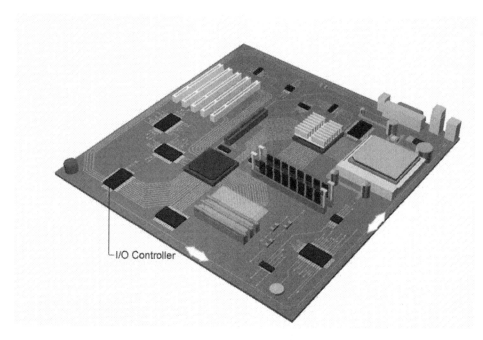

I/O Controller

 When the decoder chip produces the Hexadecimal code it is sent along the keyboard cable to the connector on the back of the computer. Once inside the computer the code goes to the I/O controller chip.

ROM BIOS

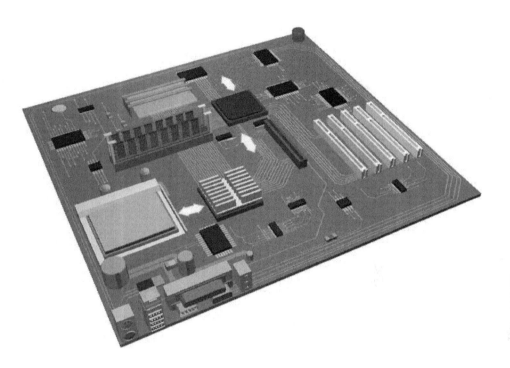

When the code leaves the I/O controller it eventually ends up at the CPU.

Here a lookup table of codes is fetched from the ROM BIOS stored in memory. An ASCII key code is found for the key that was pressed.

The code is presented to the program which is running. The program then decides what to do with it. The letter or number will be displayed, if it is not assigned to an application.

Displaying a character

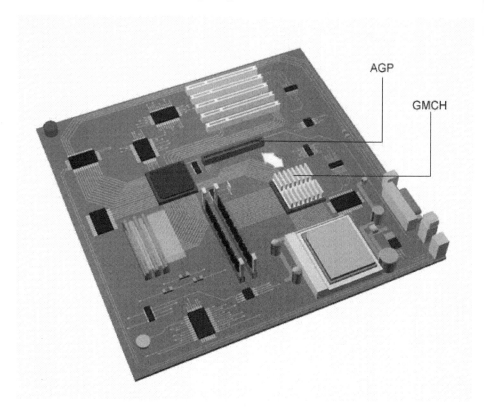

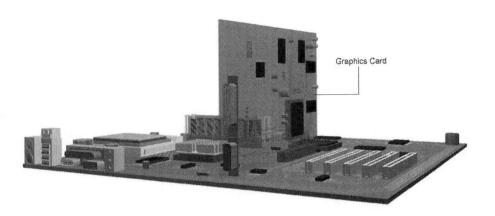

Graphics Card

The character data is sent to the graphics card. The graphics card processes the information and updates the monitor.

17. Monitor

The Monitor provides a means for displaying activity on the Windows desktop. Computer monitors come in different sizes. A 22 inch monitor is a common size; with a larger monitor the screen is clearer which reduces eyestrain. Two main technologies are used in monitors.

The LED or the liquid crystal display (LCD). The LCD monitor takes up less desk space. Here we will describe how a LCD monitor works.

Pixel

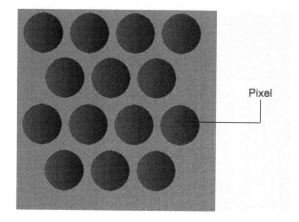

The screens surface contains pixels, the smallest area that can be controlled. Each pixel displays a colour. The pixel element is so small that it is difficult to see on its own.

On a monitors surface thousands of pixels are on the surface in rows and columns, the very narrow gap between them enables an image to be built up.

Display Adapter

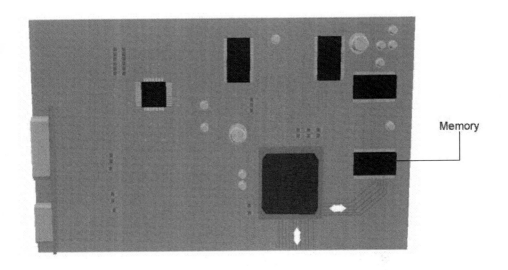

Memory

Data transfer to Memory (VRAM)

 Before the monitor can display an image it receives
information from the display adapter in the computer.
The display adapter contains VRAM memory, which
stores a colour number for each on-screen pixel.

The CPU updates the VRAM memory every time it
wishes to change the colour of a pixel. It places a colour
number for the pixel it wishes to change in the display
adapters VRAM. Each VRAM memory location
represents one pixel on the screen.

GMCH

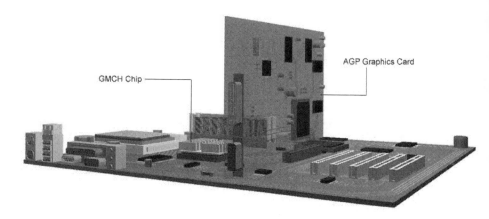

GMCH Chip

AGP Graphics Card

Data bits are sent from the CPU to the Graphics and Memory Controller Hub (GMCH) chip. The controller then routes the data to the AGP universal connector. Data is placed in the display adapters VRAM.

VRAM

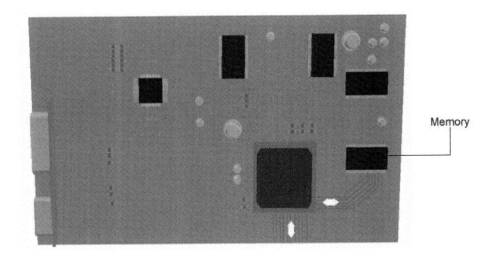

Memory

Data transfer to Memory (VRAM)

The Display adapter then reads all the VRAM address locations into a special chip which contains three digital to analogue converters one for each of the primary colours used red, green and blue.

The DAC uses a look up table to interpret the digital value to voltage that represents a specific colour. The on board VRAM on the display adapter determines how many colours can be displayed.

Super VGA

Super VGA adapters have enough VRAM to store 16 bits for each colour. This means 16,000 separate colours can be displayed.

With 24 bits a pixel can display up to 16,777,216 different colour shades (True colour).

Resolution

Pixel

The resolution is the number of pixels that can be displayed horizontally and vertically on the screens surface. These signals also set the monitors refresh rate, which is how frequently the screens image is redrawn.

18. Hard Drive

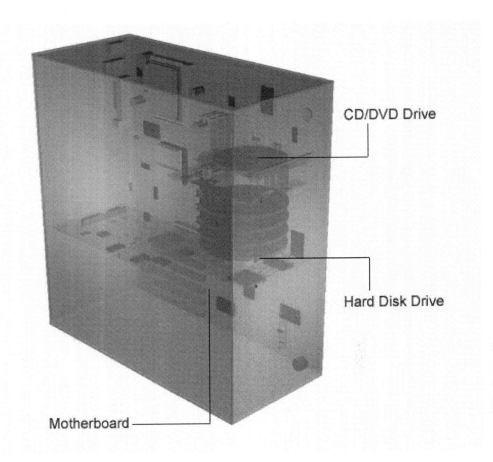

CD/DVD Drive

Hard Disk Drive

Motherboard

The hard disk drive is the primary device used for storing data. Every computer has a hard drive built into the machine. The computer's hard drive is where the operating system and most installed programs are loaded from. With its high-speed operation programs can be loaded quickly.

When buying a new computer it's a good idea to buy a machine whose hard drive has a large storage capacity and fast access time.

Drive Types

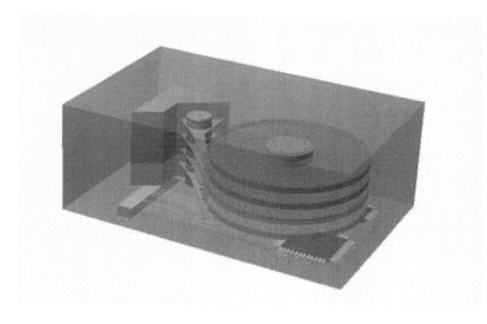

A hard drive can typically store many gigabytes of data, a CD-ROM disk is limited to 650 megabytes and a floppy disk just 1.44 megabytes. The access time governs how fast data can be retrieved from the hard drives disks.

Whereas with CD-ROM and floppy drives the storage media is not permanent, with a hard drive the disks are contained in the case.

SCSI Drive

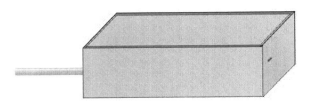

 Because of their huge storage capacity extra hard drives can be added either internally or externally. Because of its faster transfer rate external drives tend to use the more flexible SCSI (small computer system interface) interface.

Additional internal drives make use of spare E-IDE (Enhanced - Integrated Drive Electronics) connectors inside the computer.

Case

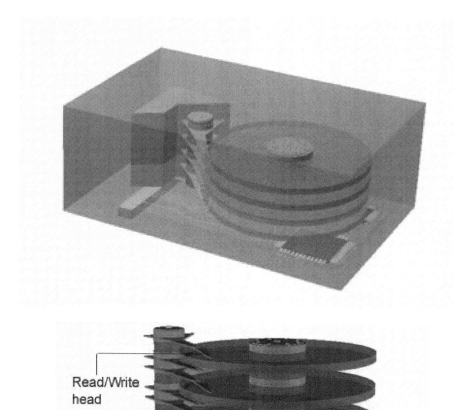

Read/Write head

Platter

The drive is contained in a sealed case to keep out dust and foreign particles, which would otherwise damage the delicate surface of each platter. On the platter surface is a thin magnetic coating. Anything trapped between the surface and read/write heads could damage the coating. An electric motor spins the metal or glass platter at speeds of up to 10'000 rpm.

The number of platters and coating composition determine the amount of data the drive will hold.

Read/Write Heads

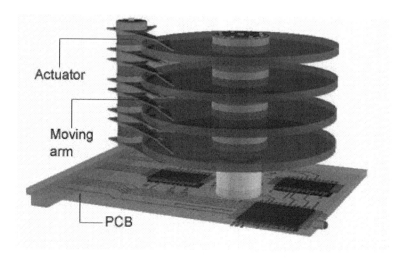

A read/write head is dedicated to each platter and the head is attached to a moving arm. An actuator positions the arm in a precise location across the platter. The head writes data from the disk controller to the platter or reads data from the platter.

Underneath the platters is a printed circuit board which controls the positions of the read/write heads enabling data to be read or written.

E-IDE

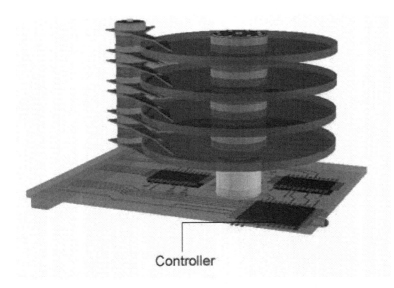

Controller

On a E-IDE (Enhanced - Integrated Drive Electronics) hard disk the disk controller receives commands from the operating system and BIOS. The circuitry translates these into positions for the read/write heads to move to and whether to read in data or write new data onto the platter surface. The circuitry has the job of keeping a constant speed for the drives electric motor.

I/O Controller

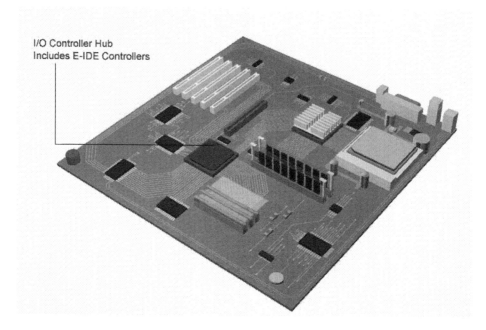

I/O Controller Hub
Includes E-IDE Controllers

The I/O Controller chip contains the E-IDE controllers. Data is routed from the I/O Controller to the Graphics and Memory Controller Hub.

From here the data is placed onto the PCI bus to the CPU.

E-IDE

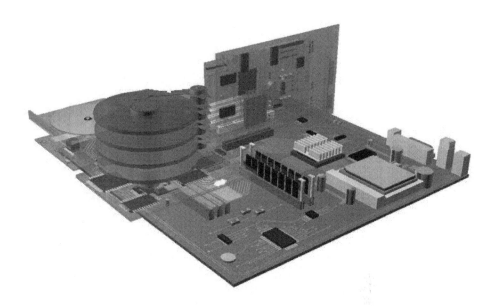

Data being read from the hard disk.

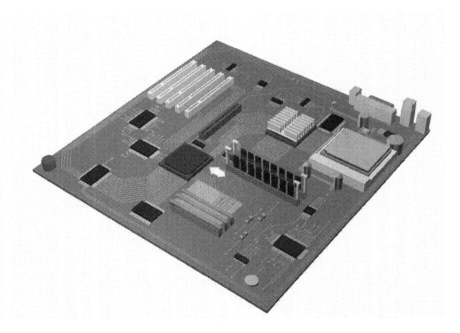

Data moves to the South Bridge.

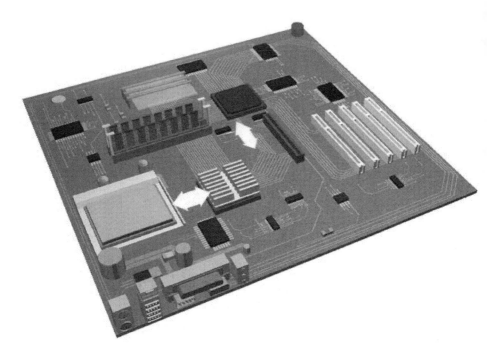

Data moves from North Bridge to South Bridge to CPU.

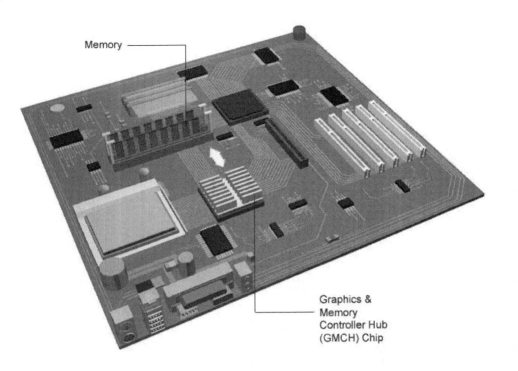

Data moves from the North Bridge into memory.

FAT

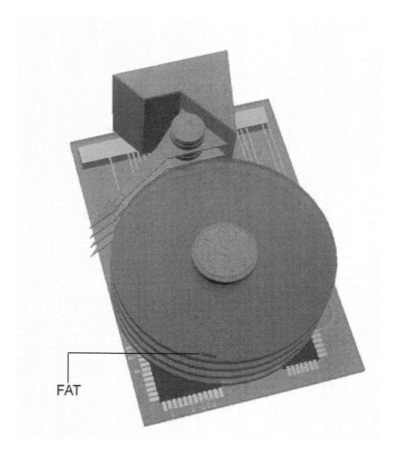

FAT

When a file is read or written, the operating system
issues a command which orders the hard disk controller
to move the read/write heads to the drives file allocation
table (FAT, FAT32, VFAT) FAT32 is the version used in
Windows XP. The operating system reads in the FAT to
determine which cluster holds the beginning section of
a file. In a write operation which part of the disk is
available to hold the file.

Clusters

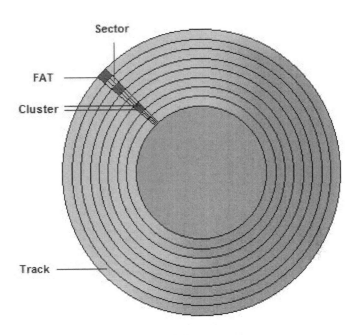

A file maybe split across many clusters so the o.s keeps a record of the cluster positions used by a file in the drives file allocation table (FAT). This file is usually stored in the first cluster(s) which are free on a hard drives platters. When a file is saved the FAT is checked by the operating system to find the next unwritten free clusters. When the FAT data has passed through the drives electrics, the operating system instructs the read/write heads to write data to the free clusters.

After this the heads are sent back to the FAT, where it writes to the platter a list of the files clusters.

Formatting

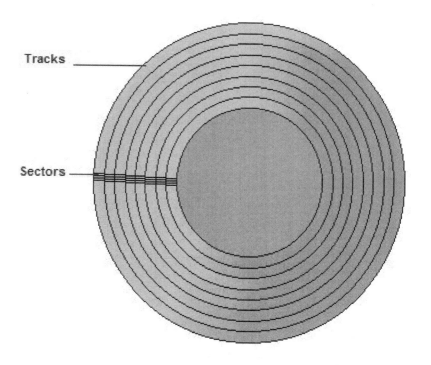

Before any data can be saved on a hard drive the disks must be formatted. This is usually done, by the makers of your computer, so you don't need to do it yourself.

A magnetic pattern is written onto the disk surface, this is so the disk controller can keep track of where the read/write heads are in relation to the disk.

This pattern consists of sectors and tracks. When the read/write heads move across the disk it can read these markers so it can tell where it is.

Disk Size

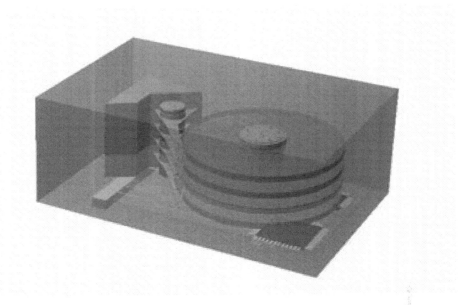

 At least two or more sectors on a single track make up a cluster or block. The cluster size varies with the size of disk and operating system used. The number of clusters that are on the disk's surface, determine the disk size.

For Windows XP or higher using FAT32.

Drive Size	Cluster Size
256MB - 8GB	4KB
8GB – 16GB	8KB
16GB – 32GB	16KB

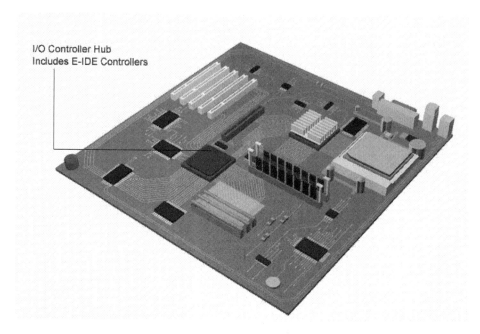

I/O Controller Hub
Includes E-IDE Controllers

Because there are so many different hard disks available, your computer includes an E-IDE (Enhanced-Integrated Drive Electronics) controller, which communicates between the computers system bus and hard drive.

This standard ensures hard drives that are compatible with E-IDE standard can work with an E-IDE compatible computer.

Virtually all PCs come with an E-IDE controller built into the motherboard.

Connection

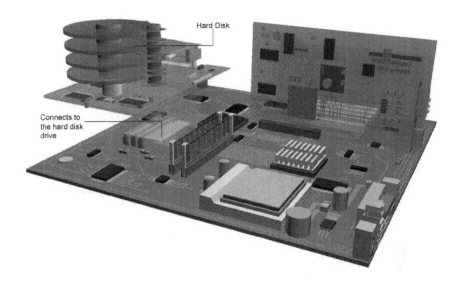

Hard Disk

Connects to the hard disk drive

From the motherboard comes a ribbon cable, which connects, to the disk drive. Up to four hard drives can be connected to the motherboard. In practice it is likely that a CD-ROM and floppy drive (where fitted) are connected to the other E-IDE controllers. If two hard drives are connected on the same cable, signals are sent to both. One drive is called the master the other a slave. The BIOS tells which drive the data is for, although both drives receive the data only one uses the data, the other drive ignores it. The E-IDE controller merely passes the commands and data to the drive in a format it understands.

19. CD-ROM Drive

CD-ROM

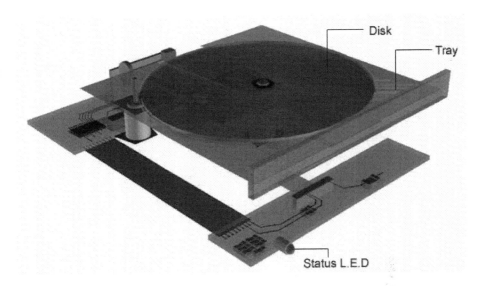

CD ROM Drive

The optical CD-ROM (compact disk read only memory) disk stores huge amounts of data, up to 650 MB on one small disk. Software programs that are not distributed over the Internet typically come on an optical CD ROM disk. The optical drives huge data storage capacity makes them ideal for storing programs, operating systems, movies and large files. Because the disks are removable the storage potential is huge.

Access Times

CD-R

CD ROM Drives are continually improving so we see faster access times and write speeds for new drives. The access time is the amount of time data takes to be retrieved from the disk.

The write speed is how quickly data can be written to a CD-R or CD-RW disk.

4x (600 Kilobyte/sec). 8x (1200KB/sec). 12X(1800KB/sec). 16X(2400KB/sec). 52X(3,120–7,800KB/sec)

CD-R CD-RW

CD-R

With conventional CD-ROM disks, like the ones your software comes on, data cannot be written to these types of disks. With CD-R and CD-RW data can be written with a suitable CD-ROM drive which incorporates a write head. Older CD-ROM drives are read only and not suitable. Data on a CD-recordable (CD-R) disk cannot be erased. A CD-rewritable (CD-RW) can be re-recorded like a floppy disk. Each CD is capable of holding up to 650MB of information.

Laser

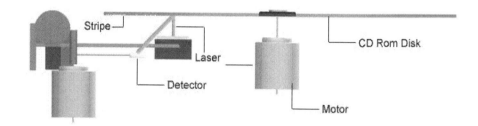

Because the laser beam can be focused so accurately mass storage is possible in such a tight space, which isn't possible with magnetic disks. A motor underneath the disk constantly varies the rate the CD-ROM rotates at.

A laser diode produces a laser beam that travels through a prism and a focusing coil.

This highly focused beam penetrates a translucent protective layer on the disk.

Disk Surface

Stripe ⌐
(Pit)

└ Land

CD ROM Disk (Side View)

The disk surface contains lands and pits. The pits are below the lands surface. As the disk rotates the laser beam is reflected from the disks surface onto a detector.

Whether the laser beam shines onto the detector is determined by the beam hitting a land section.

When the beam hits a pit the light is scattered so it doesn't fall on the detector.

Detector

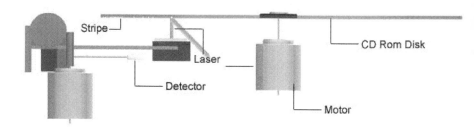

 As the laser beam light lands on the detector the light sensing diode in the detector produces a small low voltage.

This low voltage is connected to a chip which produces a stream of 1s as it receives the low voltage otherwise the chip produces 0s.

CD-R Disks

CD-R

CD-R disks are made from clear polycarbonate plastic. A dyed green colour material is applied as the first layer, with a thin layer of Gold to reflect the laser beam. Over the top a layer of lacquer and often a layer of scratch-resistant polymer protects' the delicate disk surface. During the write to disk process the write head follows an ever-decreasing circle groove called an atip (absolute timing in pregroove). In the groove a continuous wave frequency enables the write head to read this so the drive can calculate where the head is positioned in relation to the disk surface.

Writing Data

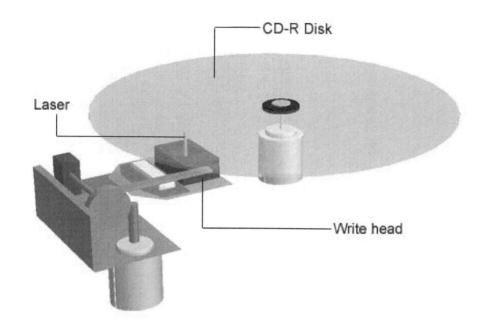

When writing data to the disk the write head follows the atip and uses the position information provided by the waves to control the speed of the motor spinning the disk. As the Write head moves towards the centre of the disk the motor must turn faster. Conversely as the Write head moves towards the disk edge the motor turns slower. The layer of dye on the disk surface is designed to absorb the light from the Write heads laser beam. When the high-powered laser beam from the Write head is switched on a stripe along the atip is made in the dye material on the disk.

Table of Contents

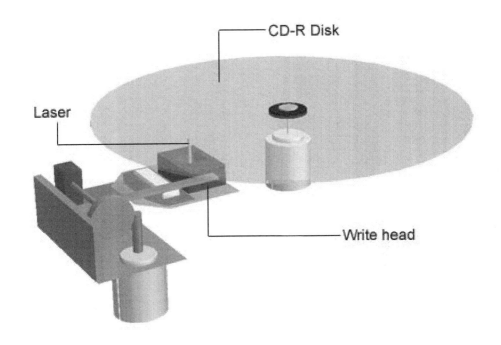

CD-R Disk

Laser

Write head

When the laser beam is switched off no strip appears thereby creating a gap between the stripes. The gap lengths as well as the strip lengths vary. The CD drive uses the varying lengths to write information in a code that compresses data and checks for data errors. The data is saved in a special format, such as ISO 9096 that creates a table of contents. This is required as there is no file allocation table like a hard drive uses.

This information is also stored on the disk.

Reading Data

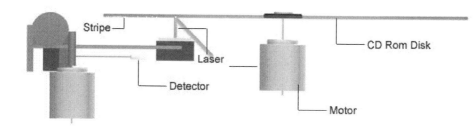

NO Data being read. Laser hits a pit

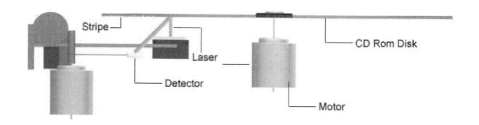

Data being read. Laser hits land

The Read head uses a lower powered laser beam than the Write head. Where a stripe is not in the atip the gold layer reflects the light back to the detector. When the laser beam hits a Stripe the light is scattered and so doesn't reach the detector.

This works in the same way as reading an ordinary CD. Every time the laser beam is reflected onto the detector a low voltage is produced, this low voltage is connected to a chip which produces a stream of 1s as it receives the low voltage otherwise the chip produces 0s.

E-IDE

From this data stream the drive decompresses and error checks the data. The drive is connected to the computer through the E-IDE interface.

The hard drive and floppy drive will also use this interface. Spare channels are available to fit an extra CD ROM drive just by plugging in the device into the ribbon cable connector inside the computer.

CD-RW

CD-RW disks are able to save data over and over again, like a floppy disk. The disk differs from a CD-R disk. The disk has a plastic base and is made up of silver, indium, antimony and tellurium embedded in it. The laser beam heats disk areas to 900-1300F.

When the laser beam is switched on the heat melts the surface crystals to a non-crystalline, or amorphous phase. These areas reflect less light than the unchanged areas. When the read head with a low powered laser beam strikes the non-crystalline area the beam is scattered and not picked up by the detector.

Reading and Writing Data

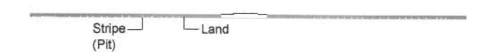

Stripe — ⌐ ⌐ — Land
(Pit)

CD ROM Disk (Side View)

These areas are pits and represent 0s. The other areas, lands represent 1s. When the laser beam hits a land the light is reflected back to the detector. Every time the laser beam is reflected onto the detector a low voltage is produced. This low voltage is connected to a chip which produces a stream of 1s as it receives the low voltage, otherwise the chip produces 0s.

With CD-RW disks the surface can be re-written by changing a pit to a land area. The annealing phase uses a low powered laser to heat pitted areas to 400F; the pit recrystallizes to its original state.

E-IDE Controllers

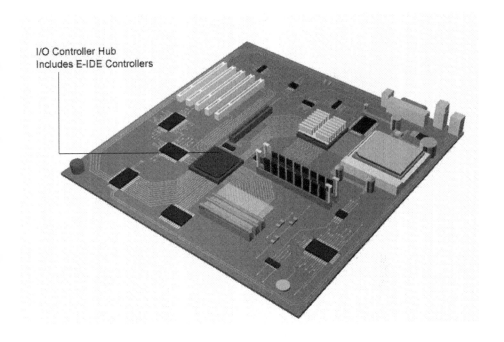

I/O Controller Hub
Includes E-IDE Controllers

The I/O Controller chip contains the E-IDE controllers. Data is routed from the I/O Controller to the Graphics and Memory Controller Hub.

From here the data is placed onto the PCI bus to the CPU.

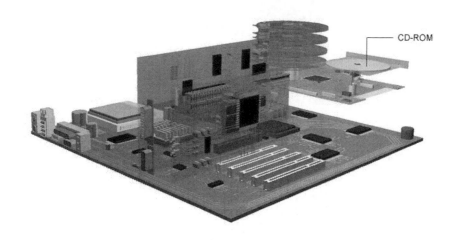

CD-ROM

The CD-ROM/DVD drive connected to the motherboard.

20. Floppy Drive

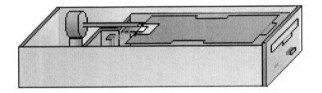

Floppy Drive

Floppy Disk

Originally the floppy disk was the primary means of transferring files to your computer. Today CD-ROM and DVD has largely superseded it. The storage capacity of a Windows formatted floppy disk is 1.44 megabytes, which is tiny, compared to the 650 megabytes a CD-ROM will hold. Hence today most software programs come on CD-ROM, as using floppy disks would require a lot of disks.

3.5 inch disk

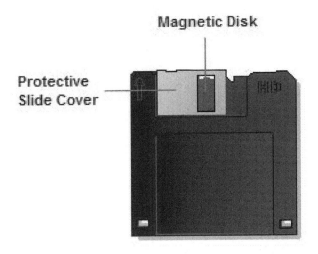

The floppy disk drive uses a 3.5-inch disk. The 3.5-inch floppy disk is enclosed in a protective plastic housing. The disk substrate is a thin Mylar plastic coated on both sides with a magnetic material. The disk can be write-protected so data cannot overwrite existing data. A small flap is moved to write protect the disk. The disk is double sided and data is written on both sides.

Formatting

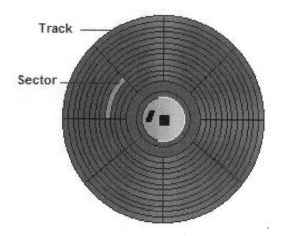

Before the disk can accept data it must be formatted. Formatting creates tracks and sectors that allow data to be organized and managed by the drive.

Tracks are arranged in concentric rings that are divided into sectors. Data written into these sectors are called clusters.

A directory stores information on what files are on the disk and their respective locations. Existing data can be erased or written over.

Inside the drive

Disk in drive shows disk surface

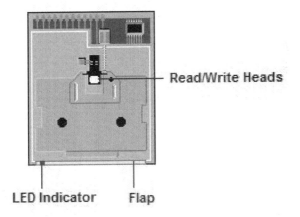

Read/Write Heads

LED Indicator   Flap

Inserting the floppy disk into the drive presses the disk against a system of levers. One lever opens the metal shutter on the outside of the disk casing. This action enables the drives read/write heads to come close to the disk surfaces. The read/write heads are located on both sides of the disk surfaces. The heads move together but are not directly aligned to each other; this prevents interaction between write operations on the two disk surfaces.

Read/Write

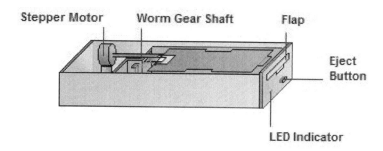

Reading and writing data is done through the same head; a second, wider head is used for erasing a track before it's written on. Underneath the disk is a small electric motor. The motors spindle goes through the centre of the disk.

When reading or writing data the motor spins the disk at either 300 or 360 rotations per minute.

A stepper motor fastened to the read/write heads moves them to the right track position.

Controller

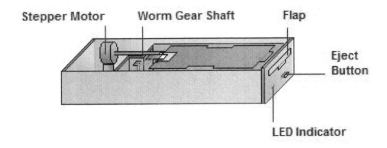

Stepper Motor   Worm Gear Shaft   Flap

Eject Button

LED Indicator

—Unprotected

The floppy disk drive controller starts the motor to spin the disk and switches on the led indicator on the outside of the drive.

When the drive receives data from the computer the drive checks whether light is visible through a small hole in the disk casing.

If light is detected from a light emitting diode shining through the hole, the drive knows the disk is write protected and refuses to write data to the disk.

Moving the heads

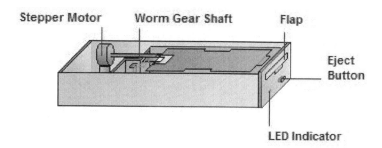

Stepper Motor   Worm Gear Shaft   Flap

Eject Button

LED Indicator

Otherwise a second motor rotates a worm gear shaft connected to the read/write heads. This movement is carefully controlled by the drives electronics so the heads are over the right track. Before data is written an erase coil on the heads is energized to clear a wide sector prior to writing data.

Inside the heads are electromagnets, which create magnetic pulses when, energized. These pulses change the polarity of magnetic pulses in the disks coating.

Writing data

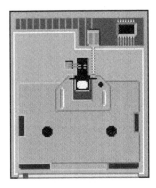

Disk inserted

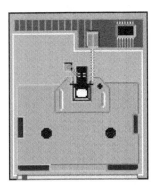

Head moved to read data

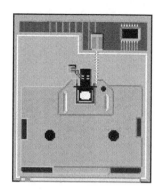

Data being read

Finally to write the data the stepper motor moves the drives head across the disk surface and writes data to the disk. The magnetized particles on the disk surface have their north and south poles orientated in such a way that their pattern may be detected and read when data is read from the disk.

The disk controller updates the disk directory with information on what files are on the disk and their respective locations and switches off the led indicator.

21. FireWire

FireWire Socket

FireWire is the name for an interface which connects devices to your PC. FireWire is particularly useful when transferring large amounts of data to the computer.

Video transfer is a popular use for FireWire.

A card for video use would plug into a vacant PCI slot on the motherboard. FireWire is similar to USB but has some important differences.

Plug and Play

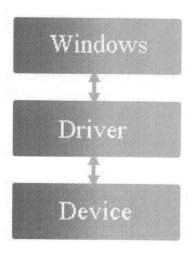

FireWire is plug and play compatible, so when a new device is connected to the computer, Windows auto-detects the device and asks for a driver. If the driver and device have already been installed the computer then starts communicating with the device.

FireWire devices are hot pluggable so they can be connected or disconnected even when the computer is running.

Addressing

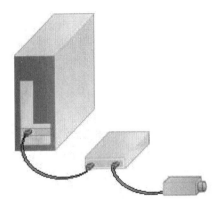

FireWire uses 64-bit fixed addressing. These are the three communication transfers, which make up the data packet when communicating to the computer.

10-bit bus ID. This determines which FireWire bus the data originated from. 6-bit physical ID. Identifies which device on the bus sent the data.

48-bit storage area. This is capable of addressing 256 terabytes of information per node. The bus and physical Ids together make up the 16-bit node ID, this means 64,000 nodes are allowed on a system.

Hop

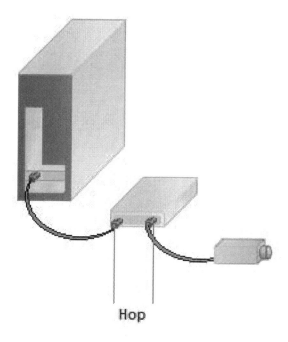

Hop

A Hop is when devices are daisy chained together. Data can travel through a maximum of 16 Hops with a distance of 72 metres. For instance a digital camcorder maybe connected straight to an external hard disk, which in turn is connected to a computer.

Bandwidth

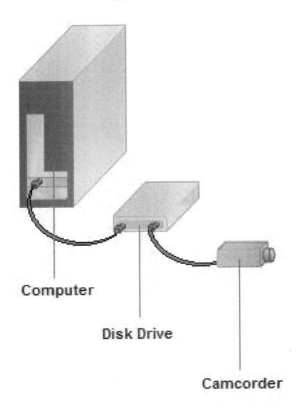

Computer

Disk Drive

Camcorder

A FireWire device can draw its power through the FireWire cable. FireWire supports isochronous devices. In isochronous mode, data travels between the device and host in real-time with guaranteed bandwidth. When a device like a digital camcorder is connected into a FireWire system it can request the host provide it with enough bandwidth for the camcorder to send the video without any disruption. With video transfer to your computer FireWire comes into its own as it enables data to be transferred up to 400Mbps.

22. USB

Universal System Bus

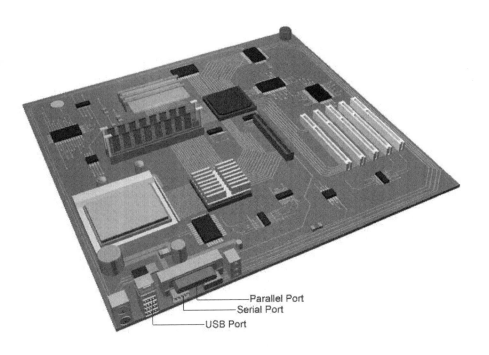

Parallel Port
Serial Port
USB Port

Although some peripherals are connected to the serial and parallel ports where fitted. The main interface is the universal system bus (USB). This allows more peripherals to be connected to the computer than the old serial or parallel ports would allow. Data can potentially be transferred at much faster rates than with serial or parallel ports. A serial port sends only 100 kilobits a second, a parallel port about 2.5Mbps. USB 12Mbps and USB 2.0 transfers data at 480Mbps. This books figures are based on the standard USB transfer rates.

I/O Controller Hub

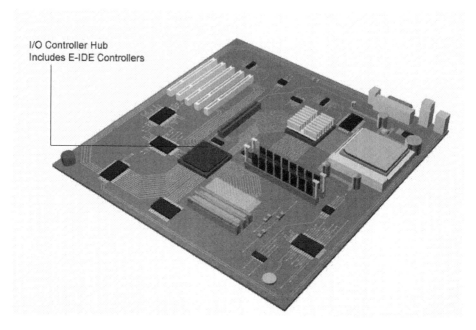

I/O Controller Hub
Includes E-IDE Controllers

On the motherboard sits the I/O controller hub, this one chip is the main hub for controlling input/output communications for the computer.

On the motherboard four USB ports are connected to the I/O controller hub. USB ports/hubs can be found on monitors or separate hubs that allow more peripherals to be connected.

USB Plug

Connected to a USB port is a four way plug which either connects to a USB peripheral /device or can attach to another hub which provides more ports for peripherals/devices. USB supports connections for most peripherals and devices, such as a monitor, modem, keyboard, printer etc.

Any of these peripherals can provide a further hub for other peripherals to plug in.

The four way connection cable uses two of the four wires to carry electrical power to peripherals /devices.

This cuts down on power supplies.

The remaining two lines, called D+ and D- are used for sending commands and data to the peripheral /device.

A high voltage on D+ but not on D- is binary 1. A high voltage on D- but not on D+ is binary 0.

USB Port

When a new USB peripheral is plugged into a port it causes a voltage change on one of the data lines. If the voltage is applied to D+ the peripheral is communicating it's a high-speed device. A high-speed device can send data at 12 megabits a second.

High-speed devices are scanners, monitors, printers and other devices that send a high amount of data. A voltage on D- indicates a slow transfer speed of 1.5Mbps that is right for a keyboard or mouse.

USB Bus

 Once the new peripheral is a member of the bus the host controller can poll the device and ask if data is ready to be sent or received and apportion the bus to the device.

Each time this happens a code is sent to the device so the host knows which device it's communicating with.

The code is sent to all devices on the USB bus.

Devices that don't match the code are ignored. Data is only accepted by those devices that match the code.

Different priorities are given to different devices.

Priority

Sound - Highest priority

Mouse - Second highest priority

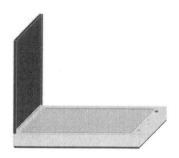

Scanner - Lowest priority

The highest priority goes to those devices that send data where an interruption in the flow of data, such as video or sound would be inappropriate. This is called Isochronous. The second highest priority goes to a keyboard and mouse where an occasional interrupt signal is received. This is called an Interrupt transfer.

A third priority, the when time permits priority, is for sending large amounts of data where there is no particular hurry for it to get there. Such as data for printers, scanners and digital cameras. This is called a bulk transfer.

23. SCSI

Small Computer Systems Interface

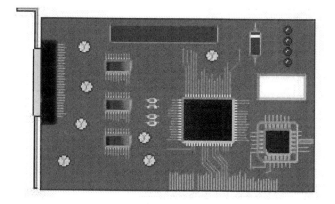

SCSI Controller Card

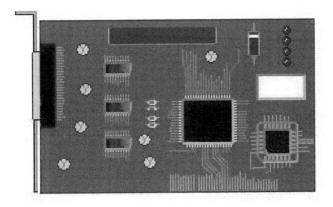

A faster way to move data between computer and hard drive is to use a SCSI (small computer system interface) connection. Typically IDE drive controllers transfer data at up to 5.5MB a second.

With 8-bit SCSI data is transferred at rate of 10MB-20MB a second.

Wide-SCSI incorporating a 16-bit data path transfers data as high as 40MB a second.

Too use SCSI on your computer a SCSI controller card is required which plugs into the motherboard.

SCSI Bus

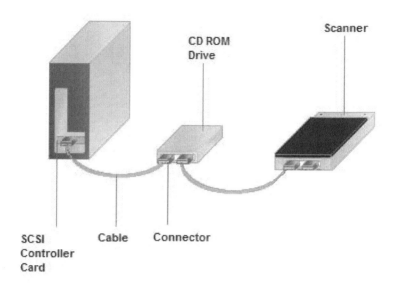

A single SCSI controller manages up to seven devices (some can run up to fifteen) like CD-ROM/DVD drives, printers, scanners and other peripherals.

These are connected through a daisy-chain connection.

We will describe how a SCSI controller card controls seven devices.

Each peripheral is connected on a daisy chain ribbon cable.

This is known as a SCSI bus.

Each device has a number between 0-6 to identify it.

Terminator

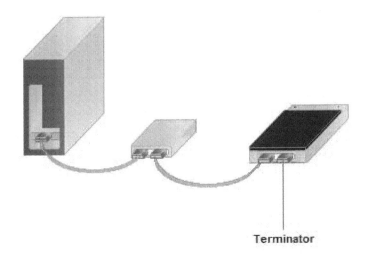

Terminator

The SCSI card usually assigns the number 7 to itself. When a device is installed a number is assigned to it, either with software, or by manually setting switches.

A terminator is the last device on the chain.

The terminator grounds the cable wiring to stop electromagnetic fields from corrupting electronic data bits travelling through.

Initiator/Targets

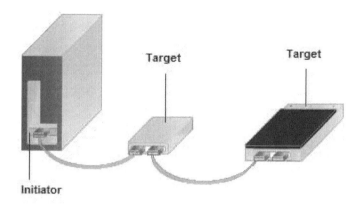

Computer is initiator

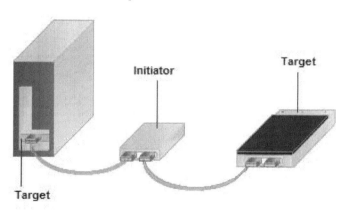

Disk drive is initiator

The SCSI bus consists of 50 wires in a cable. 8 lines
are used to transmit data and a further line is used for
parity checking. Wide -SCSI uses 16 lines, which
boosts transfers up to 40MB a second. When Windows

activates the SCSI controller card it becomes an initiator and the connected devices become targets. If a device starts communications then it becomes the initiator and the controller card becomes the target.

Arbitration Phase

Busy Line

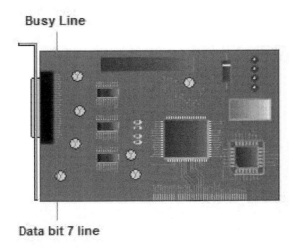

Data bit 7 line

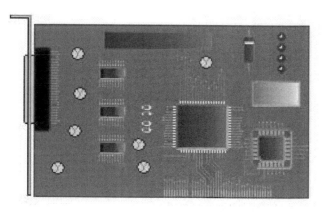

Busy and Data bit 7 line activate

To control the bus the controller waits for a pause in the message traffic and asserts control of the bus. The controller sends a voltage down the busy line and the line that carries the seventh bit of data.

This tells the bus the SCSI card wants to control the bus. During this process another device tries to control the bus; the bus goes into arbitration phase.

This process allows the device with the highest ID number to send a signal along the select line.

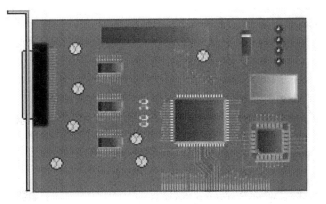

Attention line activate

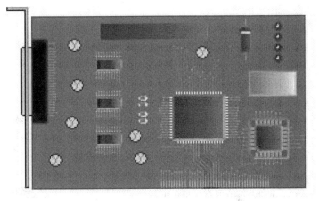

Request line activate

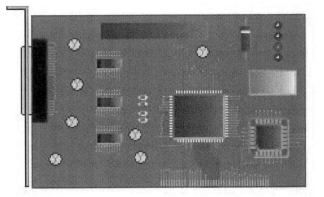

Reads in a block of data from a drive

In the selection phase the controller switches on the attention line and sends a signal to the device, for example a CD-ROM drive, it wishes to communicate with.

In return the CD-ROM switches on the request line. The controller acknowledges by placing a command descriptor block (CDB) on the data lines.

The controller switches on the acknowledge line. This tells the CD-ROM drive that the first CDB is waiting.

The CD-ROM drive then reads in the CDB and switches off the request line to tell the controller it received the data.

Data

The controller then switches off the acknowledge line to signal back the CD-ROMs acknowledgement. This exchange goes back and forth until all the data is transferred.

24. Modem

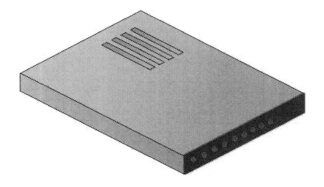

Modem

The Modem connects your computer to the Internet. Typically connecting to the internet requires you to connect to your internet service providers (ISP) modem. If your modem is external it is connected to the computers serial port.

The serial port sends data to the modem on just one line. Data is transmitted one bit after the other.

Once inside the Modem a digital to analogue converter chip converts the binary data into analogue data ready to be sent along a Telephone line to another modem.

This type of modem is called a dial up modem.

Status Indicators

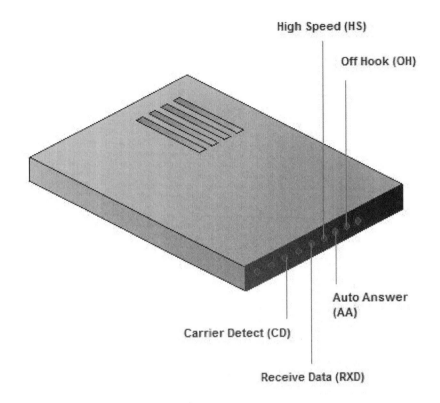

High Speed (HS)

Off Hook (OH)

Auto Answer (AA)

Carrier Detect (CD)

Receive Data (RXD)

The external lights on your Modem tell you what's going on while the Modem is working. The High Speed (HS) light lets you know that the modem is operating at its highest Transmission rate. Auto Answer (AA) automatically answers incoming calls.

Carrier Detect (CD) comes on when a carrier signal from a remote computer is detected. Off Hook (OH) comes on when the modem has control of the phone line. Receive Data (RXD) light comes on when data is received from a remote computer.

Transmit Data

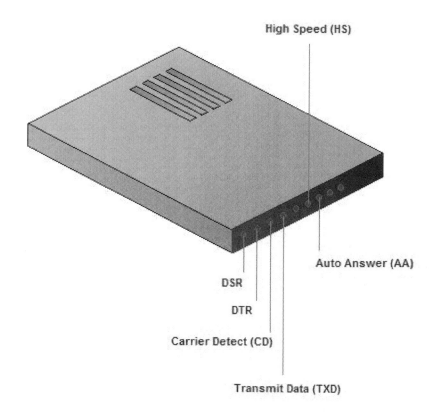

Transmit Data (TXD) light flashes on when data is sent to a remote computer. The Terminal Ready (DTR) light indicates that a communications program on your computer has issued a DTR signal.

This is typically issued when you make a dial up connection to the Internet.

When you connect to the internet you make a dial up connection, although if you have a permanent connection to the internet this is not the case. This description describes a typical dial up connection over a telephone line.

Connecting to the internet involves loading a program that handles all the protocols and communications between the modem and e-mail or web browser.

When you double-click on your ISP logo a dynamic link library called a Winsock is loaded. This invisible program is the interface between your modem and web browser and other programs you use on the internet.

Data Ready Terminal

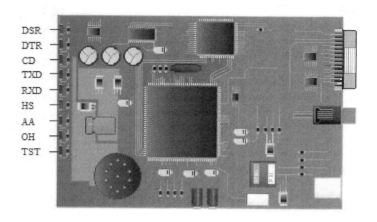

Data set ready

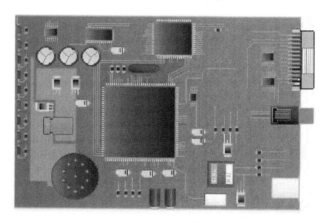

A DTR signal is sent to the modem

When you run your network connection a DTR (Data Terminal Ready) signal is sent to the modem. The DTR signal tells the modem that the computer is ready to transmit data to it. The computer also detects a DSR (Data Set Ready) signal from the modem. This command signal lets the computer know that the modem is ready to receive commands and data. If these two signal commands are not both present the modem will fail to function.

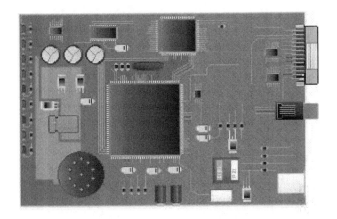

Handshake

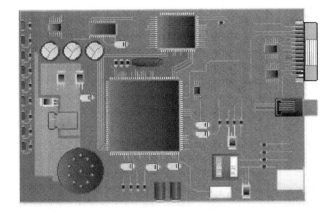

Data set ready

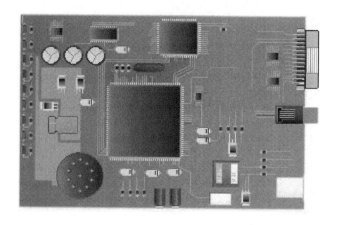

A DTR signal is sent to the modem

Once these actions are complete the dial up networking program sends out a command that tells the modem to go off hook. The off hook command is like picking up the handset on a telephone.

The next step is to dial the telephone number of your ISP. The dial up networking program sends out a command that tells the modem to dial the number. The modem responds to the command by replying to the PC on the Receive Data line.

Carrier Detect

When the modem at the isp your are calling answers the call, your modem sends out a tone to inform the isp modem that its being called. The ISP modem responds with a tone of its own.

This establishes a communication path between the two modems. Once this happens your modem sends a carrier detect signal to your computer.

This informs the dial up networking program that your modem is receiving a carrier signal that will be used to transmit modulated data.

Handshake

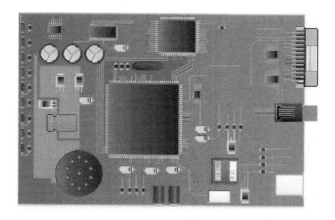

The two modems then handshake, which is a standard way of sending data to one another.

The handshake contains data such as the data transfer speed, how many bits make up the data packet. This forms the basis for exchanging data between the two modems.

With the handshake the modems could be sending data that neither understand.

Transmission Speed

1 bit

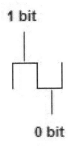

0 bit

Transmission Speed is expressed in bits per second. When the modem sends data it sends one frequency to indicate a 0 bit and another to indicate 1 bit. Analogue telephone lines cannot change frequency more than 600 times a second. Group Coding allows different frequencies to be used on the same telephone line signals. These are still sent up 600 times a second but for instance four different frequencies can be used to represent the four pairs of binary bits 0,0-0,1-1,0-1,1, enabling even more data to be sent. Data compression of frequently sent bit patterns allows shorter codes to substitute those bit patterns.

Data Packet

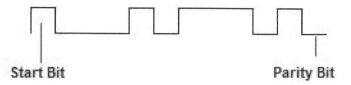

Start Bit   Parity Bit

Each data packet has a single binary bit to signal the start of the data packet called the Start bit. One or two binary bits signal the end of the data packet known as the Stop bit. To check for errors in the data packet a parity bit of either 1 or 0 is added. Both systems decide if the parity is to be odd or even parity. The data packet bits are added up by each system either 0 or 1 is added to make the total an even or odd number. Typically the data packet contains either seven or eight bits.

Request to Send

Now the modem is connected to your ISP's modem and ultimately to the internet you can send an e-mail or request a web page. To do this a request to send (RTS) signal is sent to the modem, this interrogates the modem to see if it's free to receive data from the computer. If the modem is already receiving remote data for the computer, but the computer is busy with another task such as saving a file to disk, the computer will switch off the RTS signal to inform the modem to stop sending it data while the computer finishes it task.

Clear to Send

If the modem is not busy it sends a Clear To Send (CTS) signal to the computer. At this stage the computer sends the data to the modem. This data could be something like an e-mail or web URL. In turn the modem converts this digital data into analogue frequencies that it sends over the telephone line to your ISP's modem.

If the modem cannot transmit data as fast as it receives it from the computer, the modem switches off the CTS signal, which tells the computer to suspend sending any further data until the modem catches up and switches on the signal again.

Disconnecting

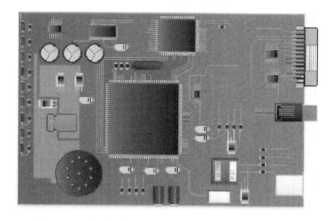

When the isp's modem hears the analogue data frequencies it coverts these using an analogue to digital convertor which converts these signals back to their original binary state.

When your internet session has finished the dial up networking program sends a command to the modem that causes the modem to disconnect from the phone line.

After this the modem will drop the Carrier Detect signal to the computer. The dial up networking program will understand that communication with the isp's modem is over.

25. Printer

Printer

The Printer allows a permanent record of a document or picture to be made. Like the computers monitor the image is built up from tiny dots on the papers surface. Whatever print technology is used ink-jet or laser, a matrix of ink dots are placed onto a sheet of paper or transparency.

Today most printers incorporate colour technology that allows high quality pictures to be printed on a desktop printer.

Motherboard

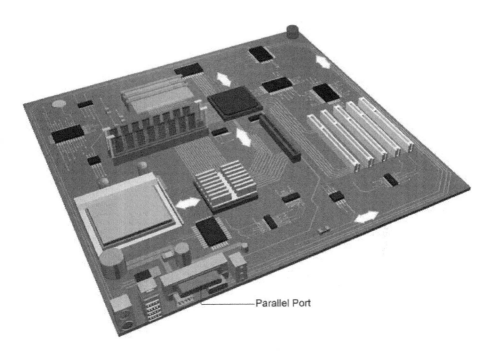

Parallel Port

Data is fed to the Parallel port

Data is sent from the CPU to the GMCH chip that in turn passes it to the I/O controller hub. From here data is routed to the I/O Controller chip.

This chip passes the data to the parallel connector.

Bitmap, Outline Fonts

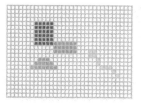

Bitmap

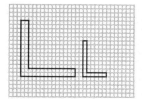

Outline Fonts

The printer accepts data from the computer in two main formats, bitmaps for the printing of images and a small number of fonts for printing text. Outline fonts are used to print a wide variety of text styles.

The printer interprets where to place ink dots on the paper page from data issued from the computer.

The Postscript format is a common type used by the printing trade.

Here the page including text is sent to the printer as a bitmap. The bitmap is a grid of dots. Outline fonts are more versatile as they allow different font sizes and styles to be printed.

Dots

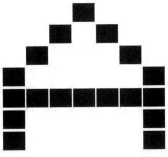

Magnified

Actual Size

A printed page consists of tiny dots positioned so close together that from a distance they appear as an image.

When you print a document or picture (bitmap) the computer decides what is the best method of printing.

With a text based document the fonts used are sent to the printer. The printer reproduces the text in the specified font.

With a bitmap picture each pixel colour is sent by the computer to the printer. The printer prints each pixel as a dot.

Print Mechanism

Small rollers move the paper vertically in time with the ink-jets print head. The print head moves horizontally across the paper. In the case of a colour printer the print head consists of two cartridges. One cartridge for colour, the other provides black ink only.

Ink Cartridge

Nozzle

Inside the cartridge are some 50 ink filled firing chambers. Each chamber is attached to a microscopic nozzle. The nozzles are visible from the outside of the cartridge.

Each chamber has a resistor which an electrical pulse travels through and heats the ink at the bottom of the chamber.

The ink boils to a temperature of 900F. The vapour from the ink expands through the nozzle to form a droplet at the tip of the nozzle.

The pressure of the vapour bubble forces the droplet onto the paper.

Character

 ─ Nozzle

Ink Cartridge

A typical character is formed by an array of these drops 20 across and 20 high. As the resistor cools the bubble collapses.

This action sucks fresh ink from the attached reservoir into the chamber.

26. Scanner

Scanner

 A scanner is a device that allows you to make a copy of a document and view/save the document in the computer. Many scanners are available, their price relates to the size and resolution that they can scan a document into the computer at.

More expensive scanners have a higher resolution (more pixels) that produces a higher quality scanned image.

CCD

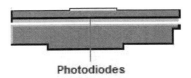

Photodiodes

 The scanner incorporates a charge-coupled device (CCD). Inside the CCD is an array of photodiodes. When light falls on them a low voltage is produced that is sent to an analogue to digital converter (ADC).

If the image being scanned is just black and white i.e. just two colours then two voltages are produced by the photodiodes.

Flatbed Scanner

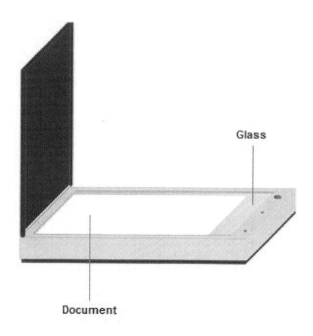

Glass

Document

With a flatbed scanner the document is placed face down onto a glass panel. The scanning processes combines shining a bright light over the documents surface.

The reflections the CCD picks up differ depending on what the light hits. Less light is reflected back off white spaces on the document.

If a colour document is being scanned red, green or blue filters are positioned in front of the diodes.

Scanning

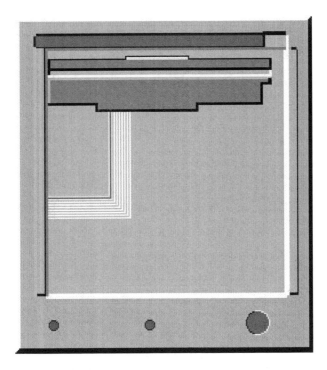

The document to be scanned is placed face down onto a glass sheet. The scanning mechanism sits below the glass sheet. As the document is scanned a motor moves the scan head beneath the page. A light source illuminates the document in the area where the scan head is positioned and this light is reflected onto the scan head through a series of mirrors.

The scan head lens focuses the light beams onto arrays of light sensitive photodiodes.

ADC

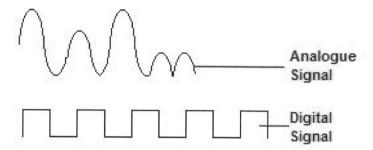

Analogue Signal

Digital Signal

The photodiodes convert the amount of light into an electrical current. The electrical current varies with the amount of light picked up by the photodiodes.

The photodiodes connect to an analogue to digital converter (ADC) that converts the electrical current into data bits that represent a pixel.

The data bits are sent to the computer where the data is stored ready to be opened up in a graphics program.

OCR

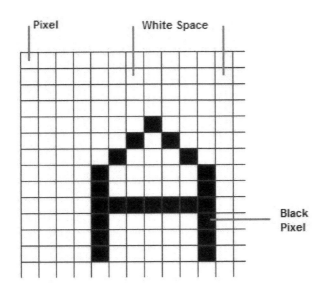

Optical character recognition (OCR) is a technology that allows text-based documents to be converted into text files. This allows the document to be edited in a word processor.

When the document is scanned, the scanner converts the dark printing i.e. the text into a bitmap. The bitmap is a square containing pixels. These pixels are either black or white. The black pixels represent a copy of the character from the scanned document. As each pixel is larger than the details of text this causes the edges of the scanned font to blur.

This causes most of the problems for OCR systems.

White Space

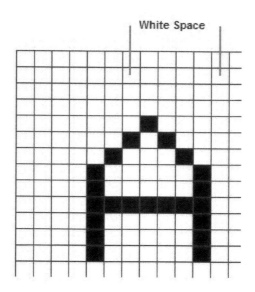

As the document is scanned in, the OCR software interprets the bitmap produced by the scanner and averages out the zones of black and white pixels. This is to map the white space on the document.

This allows the software to block off paragraphs, columns, headlines and any graphics, which may be in the document.

Baseline

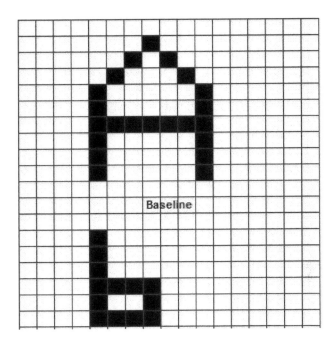

Baseline

The white space between lines is the baseline for recognizing text characters. The software's first pass tries to match each bitmap character by a pixel-by-pixel comparison to character templates that the program has in memory.

These templates include the fonts -numbers, punctuation and extended characters of some fonts.

Font

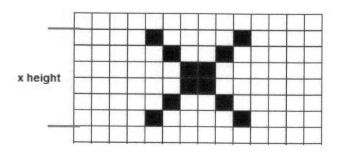

x height

To obtain a perfect match the document needs to use a font which is common to the OCR software. The document itself needs to be of high quality and blur free for accurate results.

The unrecognized characters go through a further process called feature extraction.

This time consuming process calculates the characters x height, this is the height of the fonts lowercase x.

Bowl

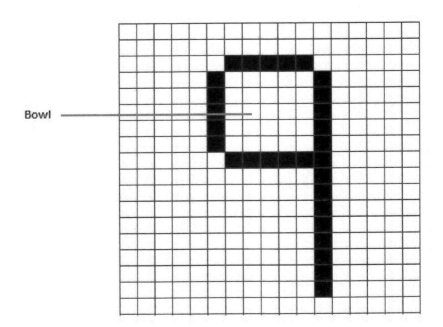

Bowl

From here it analyses each character's combination of straight lines, curves and the hollow areas within loops as in q known as bowls.

The software builds a new alphabet of the font being used which enables its recognition speed to increase.

OCR Software

 If these two processes don't recognise the character then the text character is replaced by distinctive character such as # @. From here you must manually change these symbols back to the correct character yourself. Other OCR software displays a bitmap and asks you to convert the character yourself.

The OCR software will give you the option of saving the document as an ASCII file. With this you can open the document in a word processor.

27. Sound

Motherboard

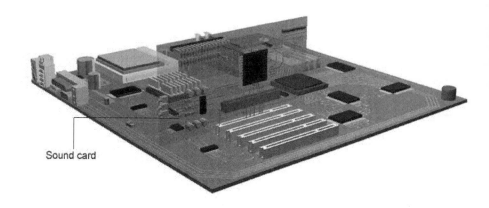

Sound card

The sound card undertakes three main tasks.

1. Converts sound from an external source i.e. a microphone into digital data.

2. Converts stored sound files in the computer i.e. MP3 files from digital data into sounds.

3. Enables MIDI instruments to connect to the computer. The sound and MIDI card plug into a PCI slot on the motherboard.

Converting Sound

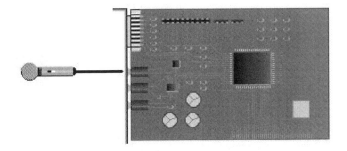

NO analogue signal being read in

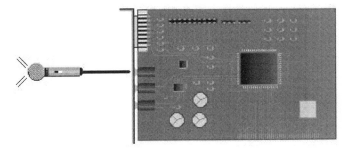

Analogue signal being converted to digital

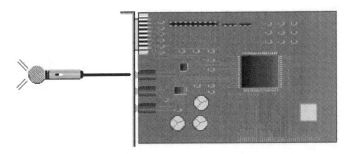

Digital data streaming out of convertor chip

The sound card converts sound from a microphone into digital data that the computer can store on the hard disk or in memory.

Converting Data

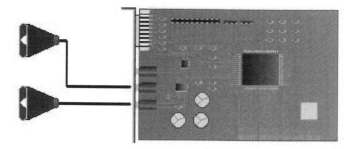

NO Data being read

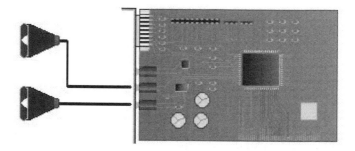

Data being read in

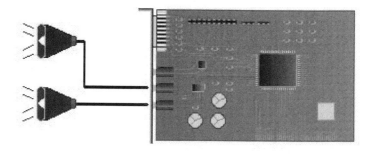

Sound is produced

Sound files such as MP3 stored on the hard disk are converted back by the sound card to analogue signals. This is then fed to external speakers for playback.

Converters

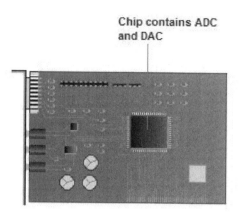

Chip contains ADC
and DAC

On the sound card is a special chip that contains an
analogue to digital converter (ADC), this converts
analogue signals into digital data. A digital to analogue
converter (DAC) converts digital data signals back to
analogue.

Data Signals

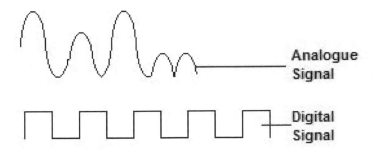

Because the computer cannot process and store analogue signals these have to be converted to digital binary data. The analogue to digital converter does this. The analogue signal is fed into the ADC and converted to binary data that represent the waveform patterns of the analogue signals. This binary data is then stored in the normal way either in memory or on disk for future use.

Analogue Signals

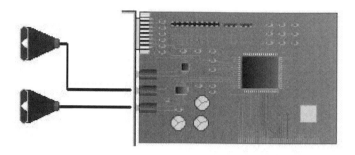

Data being read in

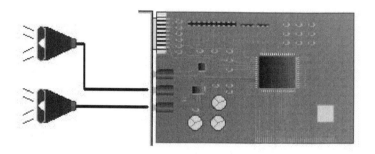

Sound is produced

When the file is ready to be played back the data is placed on the PCI bus to the sound card. The DAC converts the binary data back into the same analogue waveforms, before it was converted. The analogue signal is then fed into the speakers.

28. MIDI

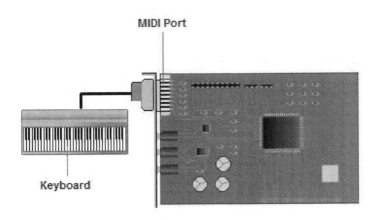

Many sound cards incorporate a MIDI interface. MIDI sound was developed to enable musical instruments like keyboards and synthesizers to connect to a computer. The MIDI system enables the computer to save instructions on how to play the sounds but not recordings of the actual sounds this is to conserve disk space.

Wave Table Synthesis

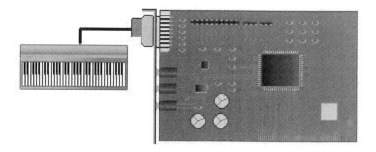

Key being read in

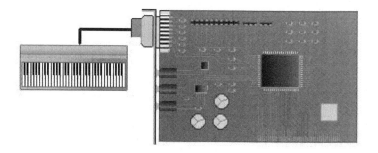

Digital data streaming out of chip

A keyboard or synthesizer issues a MIDI instruction to the digital signal processor (DSP) chip. This instruction tells the DSP which instrument to play and how to play it. If the sound card uses wave table synthesis to reproduce the sound of musical instruments, samples of the actual sounds made by different instruments are stored in a ROM chip. The DSP looks up the sound in the ROMs table. If the instruction is for a keyboard B note the DSP sends the data bits for this to a digital to analogue converter (DAC). The DAC converts the data bits back to an analogue signal.

FM Synthesis

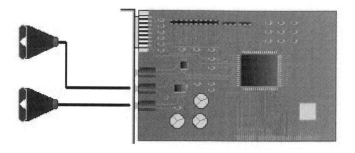

Data being read in.

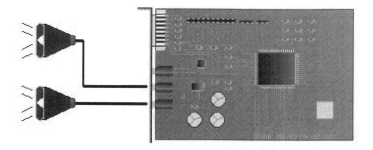

Sound is produced

When the sound card uses FM synthesis the DSP tells the FM synthesis to produce the note. The chip stores the notes of musical instruments.

The DSP sends the data bits for this to a digital to analogue converter (DAC). The DAC converts the data bits back to an analogue signal. Amplified speakers convert the analogue signal into sound.

PCI Bus Expansion cards connect to the PCI bus

Motherboard A large circuit board that contains the computers CPU and Memory. All peripherals connect to the motherboard.

POST (The power on self-test) When you first switch on your PC a test is performed inside called POST (Power-On Self Test).

This operation tests your system to make sure everything is functioning before loading the operating system.

BOOT UP A collection of programs and checks are run after the POST operation is completed.

CPU The heart of the computer, all data at one stage or another will travel through the CPU. The Intel Pentium is a popular CPU.

Memory Temporarily Stores data in memory chips that are on the motherboard. Memory sizes can be 2 Gigabyte 4 Gigabyte etc.

Hard Drive The hard disk drive is the primary device used for storing data. Every computer has a hard drive built into the machine. The computer's hard drive is where the operating system and most installed programs are loaded from. With its high-speed operation programs can be loaded quickly.

CD-ROM The optical CD-ROM (compact disk read only memory) disk stores large amounts of data, up to 650 MB on one small disk.

DVD is similar to optical CD-ROM but can store huge amounts of data.

Modem The Modem connects your computer to the Internet.

Printer The Printer allows a permanent record of a document or picture to be made.

Interrupts When a peripheral communicates with the computer it generates a special signal known as an interrupt. An interrupt is generated every time you press a key on the keyboard or move the mouse.

FireWire is the name for an interface which connects devices to your PC. FireWire is particularly useful when transferring large amounts of data to the computer.

Expansion Cards plug directly into the motherboard. This enables them to connect to local or system buses. Expansion cards are used for communicating with devices/ peripherals as data can be moved to them at a much higher speed than using USB ports.

Serial Port is provided on the back of the system box to connect external devices. Modems' connect to the port. The serial port is now being superseded by USB.

Parallel Port is situated on the back of the system box to connect external devices. Printers, scanners connect to the port. The parallel port is now being superseded by USB.

BIOS The ROM BIOS chip contains the start up code, which is used, when your computer is switched on.

Plug and Play standard was introduced to enable devices and peripherals to connect to the computer and work first time.

Mouse The device that moves the on-screen pointer and selects icons and menu options.

Keyboard Connects to the motherboard and provides a number of keys that enable letters, numbers and symbols to be inputted to programs.

Floppy Disk is a re-moveable magnetic media that stores a small amount of data.

USB universal system bus is the main way of connecting external devices to the computers motherboard.

Scanner A device that scans documents and pictures and converts them into images that can be stored and viewed by a computer.

MIDI A standard for connecting certain types of musical instruments to a computer.

SCSI Interface standard to connect external devices such as hard drives, CD-ROM to the computers motherboard.

Monitor The device that shows what is on the computers desktop.

Resources

In addition to this book you can purchase software that allows you to see the inner workings of a computer in a graphical form.

Visual PC

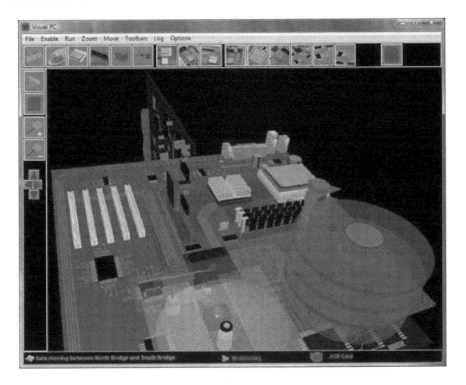

Visual PC is a brilliant demonstration of the inner works of a personal computer. The virtual reality simulations change in unison with changes on the systems motherboard, this enables a realistic demo of a computer system to be achieved.

The Mouse

When you click with computers mouse button Visual PC simulates what is going on inside your computer, with Visual PC you can see the path the data travels along on the virtual motherboard.

Keyboard

The virtual motherboard displays the data path a key press takes as it journeys to the computers CPU.

Motherboard

The Motherboard is based on a Intel Pentium processor. The board includes all the chips that would be found on a basic PC. Data flow is simulated between all the main chips. The main processes of the motherboard are simulated. These simulate data transfer between the CPU and Memory showing data flow between the North Bridge hub. The IDE interface is simulated to the CPU. CPU to AGP slot (Graphics card).

Mouse and Keyboard port simulated to CPU through LPC controller, South bridge and North bridge.

CPU

Visual PC monitors the computers processor as load changes are detected, the CPU to north bridge bus data lines turn red.

Memory Card

Simulates a Memory card with option of including operation with Motherboard simulations, so works when CPU reads/writes to memory.

Hard Disk

Simulates data being read/write from a IDE hard drive. Data is read/write from the hard drive and simulated through the South bridge to the North bridge into the CPU. This is simulated in real time when the computers' hard disk has a read/write cycle. As data moves through the controller the data lines turn to red.

AGP Graphics Card

Simulates the operation of the Graphics card including on board memory, this simulation can optionally be included with the Motherboard simulations when the CPU updates the screen memory.

Motherboard

The motherboard can be rotated and moved, you can zoom in onto the motherboard to see simulations close up. Visual PC is highly configurable you can set up the program to just monitor hard disk activity or key presses.

Visual PC can be purchased as a download from www.camboard.com

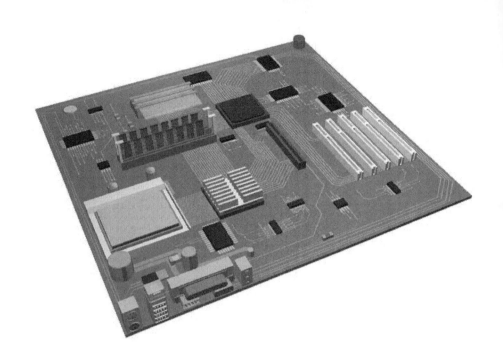

How a Computer Works

Copyright © 2015 Camboard Technology

Made in the USA
Middletown, DE
25 July 2016